PRESENT

PRESENT

The Crisis of
American
Fatherhood and
the Power of
Showing Up

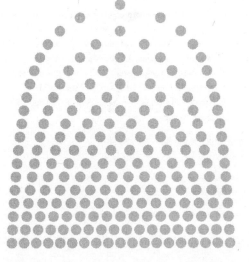

CHARLES C. DANIELS JR., PhD

CONVERGENT

New York

Convergent

An imprint of Random House

A division of Penguin Random House LLC

1745 Broadway, New York, NY 10019

convergentbooks.com

penguinrandomhouse.com

CONVERGENT with colophon is a registered trademark of
Penguin Random House LLC.

Hardback ISBN 978-0-593-73605-0
Ebook ISBN 978-0-593-73606-7

Printed in the United States of America on acid-free paper

1st Printing

First Edition

Book design by Debbie Glasserman

The authorized representative in the EU for product safety and compliance
is Penguin Random House Ireland, Morrison Chambers, 32 Nassau Street,
Dublin D02 YH68, Ireland. https://eu-contact.penguin.ie

To my wife and shining armor, Samantha

Son, Clayton

Daughter, SaMya

Mother, Frankie

Auntie, Diane

Cousin, Anthony

And the supplemental fathers who hold me close

Without you, I am nothing.

Thank you for loving me into being.

Roger, your belief in me and the love you've shown will forever echo in my heart, reminding me of the profound impact you've had on my life. I love you, my friend.

CONTENTS

Present is partly an exploration of my life's work, which includes co-founding a nonprofit organization, alongside my wife, Samantha, that helps men, especially men of color, be better dads. It's also partly a memoir, chronicling my life and how my father's absence shaped much of it. To tell this story, I relied on a number of sources in recounting moments from my life, including interviews, journals I kept during particularly challenging moments, and in certain instances, my memory alone. I strived to tell these stories as accurately as possible, as I remember them. When I've recreated dialogue, it was always with utmost care. In some instances, I have changed the names of individuals to protect their privacy. I am grateful for the grace that my family has shown me during what has been a joyful and sometimes painful process in discerning lessons from my past.

PRESENT

1. MY JOURNEY

N o young man wants to grow up to be an absent father.

As a dad to two young kids, and as a son who never had a close relationship with his father, I know this to be true.

But I also know that men never dream of being absent fathers because of my years working with men who, for various reasons, grew up to be just that: fathers who rarely, if ever, see their children. Men like my friend Sean, who, after personal struggles that landed him in jail, turned to the nonprofit my wife, Samantha, and I founded in 2011, called Fathers' UpLift.

Sean's father hadn't been around much when he was a kid, and Sean never learned how to process his emotions. He harbored lots of anger and self-doubt into adulthood, which resulted in a slew of challenges, including interactions with the criminal justice system. Following his release from prison, Sean remained captive to the shame and guilt he felt over his stalled relationship with his own children. He wanted to be present in their lives, and though he couldn't figure out how to make that happen, he had the wherewithal to know he couldn't do it alone.

Through hard work, and sometimes sheer force of will, Sean learned to forgive himself for his past mistakes. He took important steps to heal from past trauma and engaged in the hard work that would ready him to reach out to his children. It wasn't easy, and there were many moments when Sean doubted whether he'd be able to succeed. But I'll never forget the moment when Sean finally picked up the phone and made the call he had dreamed of for years.

What would he say? Would his son be angry? Would Sean be confronted with rejection? The anxiety had taken a toll and roiled him with self-doubt. He couldn't help but imagine worst-case scenarios coming true. But I stood by Sean, coaching him along each step of the journey. Practicing with him what he'd say. Preparing him for a range of responses. Giving him tips about how to process what would surely be a flood of emotions after he made that call, regardless of what happened.

The big day finally arrived.

We were sitting in my office, a phone on the table. Sean picked up the receiver and tensed up as he dialed each digit. The line rang. Sean said hello. And just like that, all the stress and fear and shame seemed to melt away.

"Dad, I missed you, man!"

Tears ran down Sean's face.

Sean told his son how much he loved him, too. How he had missed him every day they had been apart. The words didn't come easily to Sean—it's difficult to express years of love and regret and longing in one phone call—but the feelings he sought to convey flowed freely.

"I love you," Sean told his son.

There would be more work ahead. The counseling and therapy would continue. I'll talk about that in more detail later and explore the work I engage in with other dads like Sean. But in that one moment, Sean took an important step and, as a result, one more child had a father back in his life.

The relationship between sons and their fathers has been written about in many books. The lessons Dad taught, the challenges he overcame. How to love your father despite his flaws, or coming to terms with a relationship that might not have been perfect but was still important and helped make you the man you are today.

This isn't one of those books—at least not when it comes to my own life, pieces of which I'll share throughout the book. That's because my story is saturated by the lack of a relationship with my father. I yearned as a child to know deeply a man I saw just a handful of times in my life, and almost never for more than a few minutes at a time. A man who captivated my mother and who held a firm grip on my imagination. Despite this lack of relationship, my father, or more accurately, his absence, nonetheless shaped my life in profound ways.

Because of my father, with whom I share a name but little else, I sought love in places where love wasn't to be found. My longing for him caused me to lie when people asked where he was, and it's also because of him that I let anger get the better of me at different times over the course of my life.

But in some ways, it's also because of him that I earned a doctorate in clinical social work and co-founded the nonprofit organization that helps men like Sean be better dads. I have chased excellence and success my entire life, and it doesn't take an advanced psychology degree to see that some of that drive stems from not having my father in my life.

My father may be something of an unseen character in my life, as well as in this book, but he somehow still exerts an influence over me and my work in profound ways.

I have a lot to say about fatherhood and fathers, even if I can't write a whole book about my own. Instead, I remember the people who stepped in to father me when my actual dad seemed to want nothing to do with me. My mom and my aunts. My cousins and my brothers. The men at church who taught me how to tie a tie and how important it is to look another person in the eye when shaking hands. The professors, coaches, friends, and mentors who stepped up when I needed their help. These are the people who taught me lessons that I still use today in my work at Fathers' UpLift.

I will also introduce you to some of the men who have turned to Fathers' UpLift for help, and who have turned around their lives and gained the skills to be present with their children. Many of them did not have a father figure in their own lives, and thus did not have role models. But that doesn't mean they can't be good dads. Sometimes these men have been written off by society, but we always take a deeper look, applying lessons from my time in the classroom to figure out: How can we help them in their journey of learning what it takes to be good dads?

As I wrote this book, I returned again and again to my experiences in classrooms, as both a student and a teacher. The transitions I've made from student to educator, and eventually to college-level instructor and founder, have left a profound impact on my journey.

The principle that attracts me most to teaching is the idea

of lifelong learning. The value that accompanies being a perpetual student resonates deeply with me. The best educators recognize that every student ardently craves knowledge and strives to excel, even when it may not be readily apparent. I keep this belief close to my heart, and it's a mindset I bring to my work as a social worker, a CEO, and a father. In these roles, even though I'm not working inside a traditional classroom, I see myself as an educator. The subject? The art of self-parenting and fatherhood. My "students" are eager to master these subjects and succeed in their roles. For many, I might be the first teacher that ever believed they have the capacity to excel.

But what about students who aren't putting in the work or who aren't even showing up? As you'll read later in the book, I was one of those students earlier in my life. But luckily for me, one professor took time to ask me what was going on after I missed a few classes. When I explained that I was juggling life with a newborn and sharing one car with Samantha, we found solutions. I was able to keep studying. I've never forgotten that, and I try to apply the same mercy to the men who turn to us for help but who aren't always where they're supposed to be. Similarly to any classroom, men who want to be good dads may be absent for various reasons, many of which remain concealed until we take the time to understand their lives beyond the classroom. Grasping their reality is crucial in guiding them back to the learning environment they desire.

As an educator, I try not to judge or penalize students the first time they miss class. Instead, I try to understand their circumstances. This same principle shapes my work with fathers. I seek to comprehend the reasons behind their absences and understand the underlying factors contributing to their challenges in parenting. This approach serves as a means to explore diverse experiences, beginning with my own, while leveraging my perspective as both a learner and a teacher.

One of the most gratifying aspects of being an educator is realizing that your students are also teachers in their own right. As a teacher, I embrace the chance to learn from my students, whether in a traditional classroom, a counseling session, or a group meeting. Throughout this book, I present insights into the numerous educators, literal and otherwise, who have taught me, and distill these experiences down to a lesson that I apply in my work to support other fathers as they work desperately to get back into the classroom. There's no lesson I share that I haven't gained from a gentle teacher and applied to my own life.

Before getting to particulars, it's important to understand the state of fatherhood today, and the impact that not having a father figure has on children.

More than ten million children in the United States—equivalent to about the entire population of Michigan—see their fathers less than once a month. And when children don't have father figures in their lives, the results are often devastating. Poverty. Issues with emotional and mental health. Trouble finishing school. A higher likelihood of spending time in prison. And those are just the realities we can glean from statistics. Behind each statistic is the story of a man struggling to make sense of emotions that often rule his life. I'll introduce you to some of these stories throughout the book. But here are a few circumstances that we see regularly in our work.

First, fathers who aren't present in the lives of their children are sometimes survivors of horrific abuse, or have been in and out of jail so many times they can't keep track. Also, addiction is common, but how it affects their self-esteem and their relationships with their children is always unique. It takes time—months, often years—to learn their stories and to come up with a plan that will help them get their life back on track. After all, no two stories are ever the same, and thus we don't have a one-size-fits-all solution to offer.

Study after study shows that the negative impacts of growing up without a father can last for a lifetime, and are often passed on from one generation to the next. I explored some of these challenges in a journal article I published in 2023, "Evidence Informed Fatherhood Program: An Evaluation."[1] I wrote about how a father's absence due to incarceration has been linked to antisocial behavior, inappropriate behavior, early pregnancy, low academic performance, depressive symptoms, and aggressive behavior.

Think about it from another perspective. We know there are several benefits to having an active and engaged father. A father's involvement can be a protective factor against adolescent substance use regardless of gender, socioeconomic status, or the quality of the father's involvement. A father's involvement has also been linked to a decrease in behavioral problems and to positive development in children, including their social and emotional wellness and academic achievement. Plus, a father's involvement enhances cognitive development, decreases delinquency, and decreases economic disadvantages in low-income families.

But being a good father isn't always easy, especially if a man lacks role models in his own life or experiences external challenges that make providing or showing up difficult. Black men in particular face unique challenges, especially related to what we call *social determinants of health*, nonmedical circumstances that impact the quality of someone's life. Think of things such as racism, discrimination, and poverty.

Keon Gilbert and a team of researchers produced a 2016 report entitled "Visible and Invisible Trends in Black Men's Health: Pitfalls and Promises for Addressing Gender Inequities in Health."[2] In it, they revealed that the experiences encountered by Black men were positively associated with their growing mental health challenges. A typical walk in the park or call to the police station may not be that simple for a Black man. A call for protection could, unfortunately, be a death sentence. The looming anxiety and fear can contribute to emotional duress, even suicidal and death ideation.

In 2019, the Emergency Taskforce on Black Youth Suicide and Mental Health found that Black men have consistently experienced growing levels of suicidal behaviors and thoughts over the past thirty years.[3] My take on these findings comes down to the permissions we, as Black boys and men, are afforded. All too often, we are not granted permission to feel or process our emotions. The weight attached to being a male in today's society, and all the expectations that come with it, often lead to a silent and overwhelming pain. But the message remains the same: Men are not supposed to talk about their feelings. Add being Black to the equation, and the unrelenting theme of inadequacy and emotional duress intensifies.

Only by understanding these challenges, and working to overcome them, can society empower young men of color facing obstacles to be present in the lives of their children. Take prison, for example, and the impact incarceration has on children.

One study found that more than 5 million American children have had a parent spend time in prison, someone who in many cases was a primary caregiver and who provided financial resources at home.[4]

What does this mean for kids? We know that when a father

is incarcerated, his children are far more likely to become enmeshed in the criminal justice system themselves. This reality hits Black families with particular ferocity. About one-third of the U.S. prison population is Black, even though they make up just about 12 percent of the total population.[5] The reasons for this are complex and often infuriating. And in my line of work, I often meet men whose lives have been upended by the time they spent imprisoned—and who nonetheless want to reconnect with their children.

Fatherhood programs in the United States have made a difference in the lives of many men. That's why Samantha and I have devoted our lives to helping men be better dads. But considering the increase in incarceration rates, society must demand additional support for Black fathers. Cultural, institutional, and personal factors create too many challenges for these men as they work to maintain a positive sense of self-worth. This reality warrants a comprehensive approach to offering care on an ongoing basis. Granted, achieving a sense of autonomy has been challenging for these men, and even the best fatherhood programs can't completely erase these difficult challenges.

Understanding the challenges resulting from issues of self-worth, discrimination, racism, and systemic oppression is essential when considering how to help men be better dads. Through my work with men over the years, I've seen firsthand that fathering programs and counseling decrease feelings of isolation, stress, and violent behaviors, both emotional and physical. Studies back this up.[6] As do the many interactions I've had with men who have found themselves in this exact spot.

Explaining our work can be tricky. We support dads, primarily men of color who want to be present in the lives of their children. But that doesn't mean we believe in the racist myth that Black fathers are absent by default, or that Black men are incapable of being good dads. In fact, research suggests that Black men who are present in the lives of their kids actually spend more time parenting than their non-Black peers. But Black and Hispanic men face challenges, such as overwhelming rates of incarceration and systemic racism, that can make being present difficult. And those are the men we seek to work with, men who want to be present, who want to be good dads. We aim to get them back on track.

Addressing the root challenges of why the men we serve are estranged from their kids is difficult, and sometimes it feels like the need is too great to make a difference. But when Samantha and I see a man muster up the courage to dial the phone and say hello to his child, sometimes after years of being out of touch, all that work feels worth it.

The importance of fatherhood is personal for me. For most of my adult life, I've been on a mission to parent the child within me, to help him understand that the issues and contexts that kept his father from him had nothing to do with him and everything to do with his father. Later on in the book, I'll explore this concept in more detail. For me, coming to love my inner child and help him heal hasn't been easy, but it has been fruitful. I've learned to parent my inner child in healthy ways, which has allowed me to step up as a husband and father. But let me begin a bit earlier, back in my childhood, when I began to realize my father's absence and how it affected my development.

I grew up in Riverdale, Georgia, a suburb about twenty-five minutes south of Atlanta. Riverdale was solidly middle class, about 60 percent Black, 20 percent white, and 20 percent Hispanic, Asian, or something else. We lived in a single-family house, red brick, with maroon shutters and beige siding. This house was the focal point for my family, with many members of my mother's extended family calling it home, either for a few weeks at a time or sometimes for even longer. It seemed like there was always an abundance of cousins around, and I remember lots of laughter and joy—and a healthy amount of mischief—in that house. There were also questions, so many questions, about a man who wasn't there, my dad.

Sometimes the questions would come from me; other times my cousins would ask about him. These kinds of questions at home were one thing, when I was safely ensconced in the love of my mother, aunts, and cousins. When I was young, it was easy for my mother to redirect me to something else, because there was so much activity inside that house. But outside the home, those kinds of questions were brutal.

Once at recess, a student came up to me and asked pointblank: "Why's your mom always dropping you off? Where's your dad?"

My heart raced. I didn't know what to say. I froze. But deep down I knew what I wouldn't say. I couldn't tell the truth. I stammered. Told a lie. It wasn't easy. But eventually telling the lies would become second nature.

There may have been some genuine curiosity from that young student, but other kids could be mean. And not just about my dad. Even though Church Street Elementary was a diverse place, colorism was rampant. Some kids picked on me because my skin was a darker shade of brown than their own. Other kids might pick on me for talking so much about church and God and prayer, not exactly topics that build social cache among six- and seven-year-olds. So my defenses were already on high alert, and questions about my dad only made me more anxious about what awaited me at school.

Something was at work in me, even at that young age, a burning shame dwelling deep down inside me because I knew my dad should be dropping me off at school—but he wasn't. No one told me this, necessarily. But I saw how my neighbor, Roy, another kid my age, was always hanging out with his dad, putting up Christmas lights when the days grew shorter, or tossing a football around to get a leg up before the season started. Plus, some of my cousins had good relationships with their fathers. At the park, where I played pee-wee football, I saw how the other kids would glance over at their dads on the sidelines in between plays. I even had a friend who regularly rode horses with his dad. A dad and a horse! It all felt so unfair. I longed for that kind of presence in my own life.

So when a kid asked where my dad was, my hackles rose and I did what I needed to do in order to conceal my shame. I lied.

"Oh, he's a professional football player and he's too busy," I'd sometimes say.

A perfect lie. It lessened some of the bullying; no one wants to mess with the son of a professional athlete. But more important, the lie's simplicity and directness ended the line of questioning altogether. Young kids aren't exactly known for asking probing follow-up questions.

While my dad's absence forged an indelible piece of my identity, my childhood was hardly colored by a constant state of sorrow and anger and shame. Looking through old photos, I'm struck by all the smiles I see.

In one picture, taken when I was probably six or seven, I'm

dressed to the nines in a gray double-breasted suit, with a white button-down shirt and a black tie. I even have a white pocket square tucked into my jacket. I must know I look great because I'm staring straight ahead into the camera, a wide grin plastered on my small face. I think we're getting ready to head out to Midway Missionary Baptist Church, the community where my mom found the support my father failed to provide and where I looked up, literally at that age, to strong male role models. Those men weren't my father, but they sure were my dads.

In another picture, I'm sitting with a group of my cousins. We're on the floor, in front of a large speaker with wood-paneled walls behind us, and we're playing with what looks like pretend cash. We've thrown a few of the bills up in the air and the photo shows them falling back down to the ground. We all seem to be getting along, no small feat in a home filled with young kids and headed by two women, my mother, Frankie, and my Aunt Diane.

At first, it was just my mom, me, and my older brothers, Johnny and Corey. Johnny got married and moved out when I was very young. Corey, then a popular DJ in Atlanta, worked late hours and wasn't around all that much. It was actually quiet for a bit. But pretty soon, the house would be bustling again. My cousin Janice was around all the time, helping me with homework and giving my mom a chance to relax. Janice was also one of many family members who fed my seemingly insatiable hunger for books, taking time to read to me even though I'm sure I could repeat some of the stories by heart.

My mom hails from West Palm Beach, Florida, about nine hours south of our home in Riverdale. Family lore held that my grandmother, a housekeeper, had worked for the rich and powerful of Palm Beach, perhaps even for the Kennedys, we were told as kids. I remember seeing her occasionally being dropped off at home in fancy cars when she couldn't find another ride home.

Auntie Diane became a second parent, and she was a huge help to my mom. Like my grandmother, she worked as a housekeeper, which meant she could be home to help with meals and get us ready for bed. There's an African proverb, which is perhaps a cliche at this point, that it takes a village to raise a child. If that's true, Auntie Diane came close to being the mayor of that village.

I was a curious child, never afraid to ask questions. My mom says she remembers me wanting to know about my father from a young age. Part of that could have been that my two older brothers each had different fathers, with different levels of involvement in their lives. So fatherhood was a topic of conversation in our home.

Johnny, the oldest, knew his father. My mom later told me that she had been in love with Johnny's father. But he cheated on my mom, and she wasn't going to stand for that, so they broke it off. But Johnny's dad stayed involved in his life.

My other brother Corey had a father with a completely different set of challenges. My mom had actually been married to Corey's father, and they lived together for a while down in West Palm Beach. But he was an abusive man who regularly hurt my mother. Thankfully, she left him and took Corey with her.

As for me, my mother didn't exactly hide her relationship with my father, so it was natural that I would ask questions. When the phone rang, she answered, and when she heard his voice, her world ground to a halt. She would take the phone into her bedroom and they'd talk for what felt like hours. Every once in a while, which at first felt like a treat, she handed the receiver to me.

"Hey boy, how you doing?" my father would say.

"Good," I'd reply, unsure what to make of this interaction.

"Good," he'd say. "Put your mom back on."

That was more or less the extent of our conversations. Too much time has passed for me to be able to recall how I felt after those interactions, but looking back, I imagine I must have felt confused. Why were these brief exchanges the extent of my relationship with my dad?

Occasionally, those terse exchanges that took place on the phone would instead occur in person. Each summer, we'd load up the cars, stuffed full with suitcases and cousins, and begin our annual trek down to West Palm Beach. We'd sometimes stop along the way in Valdosta, a city that sits just a few hours from Riverdale, near the Georgia-Florida line. That's where my dad lived—along with his wife and children.

We would stop in Valdosta so that my mom could get some in-person time with my father. Even if they viewed their romance as magical, these rendezvous definitely were not. At least not to me or my cousins.

The visits usually went something like this: We'd pull the car into a gas station or a KFC. My father would greet my mom with a hug, then come over and see me. The conversations mirrored the ones on the phone: awkward, short, and clearly not the point. My mom and my father would go off together, leaving my aunt, cousins, and me to melt in the heat. As the minutes ticked by, our collective annoyance grew. Not only was there nothing for us to do, but we still had a good seven hours of driving ahead of us. Eventually, my mom returned, apologized, and we'd be off.

Back home, my mom kept mementos of my father in her

bedroom. A couple of photos, plus some football trophies. Those proofs of his athletic prowess may have served as the basis for my lies about where he was when kids at school would ask, and probably even motivated me to put on shoulder pads and hit the turf when I got a bit older.

I eventually stopped asking so many questions about my father. There's only so many times a kid can hear his mom say that his dad is too busy to see him before he decides he's had enough. That message morphs into, *My dad would rather be doing other things than spending time with me.* Those internal messages quickly grow even darker and more damaging: *If only I were better, my dad would want to see me. It's my fault he's not here.*

The self-doubt stemming from my father's absence made me an easy target for bullies. I became disagreeable, picking fights and trying to push people away from me. As I entered adolescence, these feelings of worthlessness only intensified, culminating in a desire to put an end to them in any way I could. Later on, as an adult, these feelings of worthlessness and inadequacy would come to dominate my thoughts—and would take years of struggle to overcome.

My goal with this book is to show, through examples from my own life and through the stories of men we've worked with, that even when a father is not present, it's possible for families and communities to step up and provide the love and kindness kids need to thrive. At the end of each chapter, in a nod to my belief in the importance of lifelong learning, I'll offer a short lesson or reflection to consider how we can support dads, or, as I've come to think of them, students who are learning the art of fatherhood.

Lesson: What if we embraced the idea of seeing every parent as a lifelong student? Let's honor the energy, knowledge (both internal and external), and diverse experiences that each parent brings to the table.

2. FATHERLESSNESS DISORDER

Cody, a young man discharged from a local hospital after being treated for suicidal ideations and violent behavior, recently came under my care. It didn't take long for me to recognize Cody's symptoms, the result of what I call Fatherlessness Disorder. Cody's mother was concerned about her son's well-being, but she didn't know where to begin. I remember the look in her eyes as she described her son.

"He was drinking a lot, got into a lot of fights, and was talking about killing his father," she told me. "He always asks me why his father wants nothing to do with him. He's now sixteen years old and has never met him." Her voice trailed off. "He wants to see his father so bad . . ."

I agreed to work with Cody, and together, he and I struggled with making sense of his father's absence and how, as he put it, his dad "wanted nothing to do with me."

He desperately begged his mother to continue reaching out to his father's family. But each time she did, it would take days or weeks for him to reply. The wait each time was excruciating for this young man. He responded by lashing out with outbursts in school, drinking to excess, and undertaking a constant search for validation in unhealthy ways.

We worked to separate the choices of Cody's father from who he was, which wasn't dependent on how his father had mistreated him. The two were intertwined and caused severe injury. But I helped this young man understand who he was, to untangle his identity from his father's choices. He could then begin to believe that he shouldn't blame himself for the actions of another person. It was only by accepting this reality that healing could begin to take place. The young man's drinking decreased substantially as he worked on understanding how to care for himself through a series of interventions.

In one of the most surprising moments for this young man, his father actually responded to his mother's request for him to meet his son, and a time and place was arranged. I remember my meeting with this young man prior to him seeing his father.

He told me, "I will forgive my father because I know how valuable I am today . . ."

This touched me deeply and taught me two things that apply to a wider understanding about how young men heal from not having fathers in their lives.

First, pain is normal, and we can learn to live with it if we understand its origins. Second, healing takes place when we can separate the things that others have done to us from how we see ourselves. This young man blamed himself for his father's choices—and he wasn't able to heal until he accepted that his father's choices had nothing to do with him.

Whether a father is physically or emotionally absent, or both, his lack of presence looms large over his children's lives.

It's taken me a long time to learn that, but once I did, I could begin my own journey of healing. Over time, my life's work has focused on helping others begin their own journeys. Professionally, I'm particularly interested in understanding what a father's lack of presence does to his children over the course of their lives, and in helping men confront the challenges that keep them from being present in the lives of their children.

On that first point, the phenomenon of fatherlessness and its associated health risks must be taken seriously. The stakes are too high, both for individuals and society as a whole. *The Diagnostic and Statistical Manual*, a reference book that covers mental health challenges, describes about three hundred different disorders, but there is no diagnosis that describes the mental duress children and adults experience from not having an involved and present father.[7]

I've already explained that real damage occurs when a father is absent, which often begins in adolescence but which can follow a child well into adulthood. The symptoms that are associated with this reality comprise the condition I've coined Fatherlessness Disorder. These symptoms surface regularly in my work with individuals who have struggled living with father absenteeism.

The symptoms of Fatherlessness Disorder include emotional pain, such as prolonged anger or sadness and bouts of depression, sometimes brought on by feelings of worthlessness. Projected anger, manifested either externally, such as violence against others, or internally, such as thoughts of suicide, is often present as well. A man or a woman who grew up with an absent father might also spend a good chunk of their adult lives searching for a father figure. For men, this might mean seeking father figures in groups that might not always be healthy for them, such as in gangs. For women, perhaps they will seek a father figure in their relationships with romantic partners.

I know this to be true because I've experienced many of these symptoms myself.

Having grown up without my father present in my life, imprinted in my DNA is a sense of worthlessness, something I have come to regard as dangerous and soul-crushing. At the root of this feeling is an inner child who continues to blame himself for his father's absence. Regardless of age, we each carry an inner child that requires validation and care. Recognizing this inner child is essential for emotional well-being. Acknowledging that our emotional needs don't disappear as we age is critical. By identifying and addressing the needs of our inner children, we cultivate a greater sense of emotional well-being and inner harmony. This understanding allows us to approach our emotions with compassion and empathy, leading to a more fulfilling and balanced life. I'll return to the concept of the inner child throughout the book, highlighting the fact that unresolved pain and trauma from childhood can grip our current realities if it goes unacknowledged.

For me, my inner child never grew up. Instead, he wedged himself inside my psyche, hurt and scared, where worthlessness joins anger and sadness, ravaging my soul. My inner child's pain eventually became unimaginable. By the summer of 2008, my inner child's cries had become unbearable and led me down a dark path of despair, culminating in thoughts of taking my own life. The symptoms of fatherlessness loomed over me, a toxic shadow that seemed intent on snuffing out my light.

Fatherlessness Disorder continues to harm others, through thoughts of suicide, actions that lead to incarceration, unhealthy decisions that lead to unplanned pregnancies, and, for too many, unresolved anger that leads to physical and emotional abuse.

Scientists believe that when human beings experience pain, neural pathways are created in the brain and then rarely leave.[8] That doesn't mean healing is impossible, but it takes time and effort and expertise. I've experienced healing in my own life, and I've seen many other men who I've worked with experience it in theirs. But the scarring is real, and the original wound—a father's absence—will continue to harm a child if he or she can't access the resources to understand they were not at fault.

We cannot effectively bolster and support fatherhood without addressing fatherlessness. As a therapist, I realized that some form of closure was needed for me to move on from my fatherless childhood so that I could grow in my own life, especially as it relates to being a father to my own children. I had to seek out opportunities to separate myself from my father's decision to separate from me. This is an ongoing process, but without the insight that therapeutic tools can bring about healing, I might never have begun to heal. That healing was made possible because I learned about the importance of self-parenting, the notion that men need to learn to care for themselves, to acknowledge their own pain and learn how to heal, before they can be good parents to their own children.

At the beginning of this chapter, I mentioned Cody, the young man whose struggles with suicidal ideation were, I instantly recognized, related to Fatherlessness Disorder. It took a lot of hard work, but today, Cody loves himself, and he's made strides toward his goals of graduating from high school and attending college.

Cody's mom sent me a picture of him and his father together for the first time ever with the following message:

Hi Charles. Wanted to tell you Cody met his Father last night. They spent 3 hours together playing pool and talking. He told him he wasn't angry anymore and that he forgives him. He has come a long way. You were part of his journey and helped him face this.

> **Lesson:** Each student, or in our case, each father, behaves differently in the classrooms of life. There are things they enjoy and dislike. There are also fears and triggers. Fathers' UpLift is like a classroom—and there is no Fathers' UpLift without love. Each student is worth being loved despite what they bring into the classroom. How do you create a loving atmosphere in the classrooms that comprise your life?

3. WHY FATHERS' UPLIFT

There are many reasons a father might turn to Fathers' Up-Lift for help in reconnecting with their children, and we'll explore some of them later in the book. But before we get too deep into that, I want to address a concern I sometimes hear from well-meaning folks who hear about our work: What about moms? After all, moms often bear the brunt of responsibility when it comes to raising kids without the help of the fathers. Truth be told, society demands too much of moms generally and single moms particularly. Collectively, we should demand that society do more to help. So, while we serve fathers in our work, we also empower moms. That's because moms are the ones who often approach us to ask if we can help their children reconnect with their dads. Women often play a critical role in helping the men we work with take the initial steps they need on their journey of healing. And I've seen this reality play out many times.

In addition to obvious stressors, such as trying to raise a child on a single income or not having enough time in the day to get everything done, single moms often face complex and often invisible challenges. When a kid struggles in school, it may be difficult for a single mother to advocate for her child, especially because overburdened institutions may need the kind of follow-up that is only possible when an entire community is backing the child. When moms need some help, we're there for them as well. Let me explain.

My wife, Samantha, is an irreplaceable partner in our work at Fathers' UpLift for many reasons, and her gifts shine through perhaps most brightly when she's working with some of the many moms who seek us out. Often, our moms want to help their sons whose longing for relationships with their fathers creates challenges in their lives. No story is the same, and Samantha's ability to cut to the core of what each woman is facing helps her to find the resources that will most benefit the mom. But one story has stuck with Samantha for years, and it helps shine a light on how our mission benefits not only dads, but moms and entire families.

A mother of several children approached Fathers' UpLift because her partner was abusing drugs and alcohol, and, like so many people, he had become addicted to opioids. The mom, Cheryl, needed support. Her partner was not the biological father of most of her children, and while she had extensive histories with her children's birth fathers, they hadn't stayed present in their lives for very long. But this man, despite his challenges with substance abuse, had become an integral part of Cheryl's family. She wanted to get him the help he needed in order to stay connected to their blended family.

Samantha helped Cheryl early in their counseling sessions to cope with the challenges accompanying her partner's several attempts at rehab. But within a few months, Cheryl received a terrible call that her husband had overdosed and died. Samantha realized pretty quickly that Cheryl was a mom who needed support in raising her children. So she helped Cheryl find a way to work through the grieving process while simultaneously connecting her to support services for herself and her children. While Cheryl had come to Fathers' UpLift looking to learn how to support herself and her partner, she ultimately ended up working with us to overcome her grief caused by his death.

Samantha told me that Cheryl's story reflects the experiences of many of the mothers we are privileged to serve. Moms who come to us usually seek our help not for themselves, but for the fathers of their children. Samantha often hears the pain and frustration in their voices when moms ask her questions like, "How do I get the fathers back into our children's lives? How do I get them sober? How do I get them some help? What can I do? They have done everything that they can, and nothing is working . . ."

With Samantha's insight, we've created youth enrichment services, where moms can arrange access to vital services for their sons at the same time they are beginning the healing process for themselves.

"Our entry point is at the intake when they are talking about their sons who are struggling with their father's absence, and we then acknowledge that it is hard and it seems like they need some support as well," Samantha reflected. "They say yes and begin the work right then and there."

When I asked Samantha what she thought of our work, she summed it up in a helpful and succinct way.

"Dads are essential to mothers because there is a connection that a child gets from a father figure or father that we moms can't provide, or replace, even if we tried," she told me. "And sometimes it's hard for us as moms to say that."

Samantha recalled that sometimes when she needs a break

from parenting, she will tell our son, Clayton, or our daughter, SaMya, "Go ask your dad." Before long, our kids were coming to me on their own, which prompted Samantha to wonder, "What's changed?" She said it was then that she realized I was able to give our children something she couldn't, which is partly why we're such a great team.

Of course, as Samantha rightly points out, every dad is different. Some dads can teach their kids how to throw a ball or fix a car, while others might be more inclined to read books or introduce them to old movies. But dads who are present are usually able to find something to pass on to their kids, even if it takes some time and patience.

Samantha told me that she had a moment of insight when we were interviewed by the author and radio host Tavis Smiley back in 2022.[9] She remembers being asked what it was like to be married to a man who grew up without a father. The question initially threw her for a loop.

"I have learned that I cannot be [his] therapist. I can't fix the past for [him]," Samantha recounted. She also said the question prompted her to be patient with me, recognizing that there might be things she wishes I could teach our children that just aren't possible, because my dad wasn't around to teach me.

"Not every man is the same, and we have to be okay with that," she told me.

Samantha is grateful that our children are growing up in a stable, two-parent home, but she also recognizes that no two families are the same, regardless of how they might look from the outside. That realization prompted her to ensure that Fathers' UpLift responds to a variety of familial situations. Sometimes a single mom seeks us out for help with her son, or maybe a single dad feels overwhelmed by raising children on his own and needs access to therapy. We've worked with same-sex couples who want to ensure that their kids are doing okay and even with families who, from the outside, look like ours, but who maybe need help navigating complex emotional needs.

"Human beings are not robots," Samantha said. "Nonetheless, there is always room for empathy, understanding, and love—and we provide that each time."

Sometimes Samantha and I encounter people who look at our work with suspicion, because of our focus on fathers rather than mothers. When we probe a bit, we hear a variation of the same theme: Working to empower men to be better fathers somehow, in this view, undercuts the heroic efforts single moms make to provide for their kids. But this couldn't be further from the truth.

Nothing we do at Fathers' UpLift bashes or undercuts women and single moms who are heading their households and doing badass work. In fact, both Samantha and I understand to our core how much of a sacrifice single moms often undertake to raise their kids.

"We would not be here if it were not for our badass single moms," Samantha told me recently. "They have given us something that our dads can't give us. And no one, male or female, can take that away from them."

But why can't recognition and support for moms coexist with the realization that many men are in need of help when it comes to parenting?

We think they can. Some of our strongest supporters are mothers. They don't feel undercut or ignored by our work, but instead, they see us as allies.

"They are sending us the father, they are opening the door, they are breaking down the maternal gatekeeping so the father has access to their child," Samantha told me about her experiences working with moms. "They are working alongside us to ensure that the father has access. They are giving the fathers grace—not society, the mothers."

To put it another way, we are uplifting the fathers while simultaneously uplifting the mothers.

Lesson: The great thing about helping others is that anyone, regardless of gender, can join in understanding why someone skips class. Everyone has a reason for caring about the other person in the classroom, and every reason matters, especially when we are all trying to do our best.

---

4. WHO PICKS UP THE PHONE FIRST?

"Where's my father?"
Like I said, this was a question I asked my mom over and over and over again, to the point where she'd grow exasperated and tell me to knock it off. But perhaps even more importantly, it was a question that I asked myself. Constantly. Did my dad leave because of me?

Later on, as an adult, I developed more nuanced feelings about how my mother managed her relationship with my father, and what that did to me as their child. Some folks have said that in the way I tell my story, I have absolved my mother. That may be true. But letting someone off the hook should never be a passive act. For me, it is a conscious decision to accept and acknowledge my mother as a human being, which includes flaws and imperfections that, like with anyone else, exist alongside her positive traits. I choose to coexist in an imperfect world as an imperfect person who loves his imperfect, amazing mother. But back then, I didn't have the skills to think through my feelings in this way. Instead, I turned my pain inward, blaming myself for my father's absence.

Once the seedling of that thought developed, it didn't take long for it to burrow deeply into my mind. Deep down, I just knew it was true. No matter what other people told me, what I told myself held more sway. And I told myself that I was somehow deficient. If only I were smarter, faster, kinder, stronger—or whatever -er crept into my mind at any particular moment—my dad would be around. I'd be happier. And so would my mom. Blaming myself for my own sense of loss when it came to my dad was one thing. But thinking that I'd somehow caused my mom's was another.

I'm not sure if this was better or worse than total abandonment, but my father wasn't completely absent, even after he stopped coming around regularly. My mom left, on occasion, to meet my father. She drove several hours, despite the fact that her epilepsy meant such a journey could be disastrous for her. I knew about these trips because, on the rare occasions when she couldn't find a babysitter, she brought me along. That meant her own safety was at risk—and so was mine. The visits were an opportunity for my father and my mother to rekindle whatever romance still existed. I'm not sure if I grasped, back then, what was going on. But I knew that my presence was unwelcome. That I was in the way. That I was unwanted.

As I grew up, especially in my teenage years, I wondered, What was it about this man, who had abandoned my mom and me, that kept her going back? Even risking her own life, and mine, to see him?

My father's absence affected me in ways that I'm still trying to understand, but his decision to keep me a secret has repercussions beyond our relationship. When I learned that my aunts and uncles—his siblings, their partners—and my cousins knew about me, long before I discovered them, I was hurt and confused. How had they allowed my father to keep me a secret? Were they condoning his behavior? Did they ever suggest he should do the right thing and bring me into the wider family? One of my older brothers later told me that the general rule was "to stay out of Dad's business." But his business was my business, and it stung that no one seemed to share that view but me.

My father's decisions also affected my relationship with the one person who I thought I could trust over everyone else: my mother. With the benefit of hindsight, I am able to see the complexity of my mother's choices, and I've come to accept that she has a deep connection with my father. She calls it love. But back then, when I was a child longing for my father, I saw in my mother's choices a kind of betrayal to me. She would meet up for romantic rendezvous with my father, leaving me to wonder why Momma and I weren't good enough for a house, a wooden fence, a nice front yard—and to have this man a permanent fixture in our lives. Why were Momma and I not good enough for the things that lots of kids take for granted?

As a lonely child, I thought Momma's love protected me. However, that same love is one I now recognize as having harmed both her and me. The allure my father held over my mother only reinforced the narrative I had created, the one that said the fact that he wasn't around meant he didn't want to see me. That it was all my fault.

Back in 1965, then Assistant Secretary of Labor Daniel Patrick Moynihan published a report that sought to explain the seemingly intractable levels of poverty afflicting African American communities in the United States. In *The Negro Family: The*

Case For National Action, aka the Moynihan Report, he argued that high rates of unemployment and dependence on social welfare programs in Black communities were the result of weakened family structures, particularly among poorer African Americans, circumstances that traced their roots back to the horrific legacy of slavery.[10]

Among the many evils of slavery in the United States was the routine destruction of families. Husbands and wives sold to different plantations. Children ripped from their parents. The cruelty lasted longer than the institution itself, its aftereffects still visible today.

Statistics show that as many as ten million children in the United States live in homes without their fathers. Dig a little deeper, and the numbers reveal that Black and Hispanic kids make up a disproportionate percentage of these children relative to the overall population. This isn't a new phenomenon. It's been true for generations and has roots in the evils of slavery that still persist in too many realms of life today.

Statistics like this also have the harmful effect of creating a widely accepted narrative that Black men not being present in their children's lives is normal. More perniciously, that it's the result of young men of color shirking responsibilities to their families. My work with hundreds of these men has shown me that this assertion simply isn't true. We seek to disrupt systemic racism by addressing one of the most deeply embedded, damaging, and negatively impactful effects of racist policies, practices, and environments: the separation of the Black father from his family. There are as many reasons that a man is not present in the life of his children as there are dads wishing they could be. But that false notion, that they simply don't care, has been around for generations.

Though dated, and many of its central assertions challenged

in the years following its publication, the Moynihan Report nonetheless offers helpful insight into the challenges that faced Black families, especially Black men, following the abolition of slavery in the United States. During Reconstruction, the emergence of Jim Crow laws targeted African Americans broadly, but Black fathers specifically.

"Of the greatest importance, the Negro male, particularly in the South, became an object of intense hostility, an attitude unquestionably based in some measure of fear," wrote Moynihan, whose own upbringing was shaped by the absence of his father, who had left his family when he was a child. "Unquestionably, these events worked against the emergence of a strong father figure."[11]

As time progressed, many African American families overcame a deck stacked against them and entered the middle class, with strong families intact. But understandably, many others did not. They were subject to vicious racism and systemic obstacles that manifested in discrimination in housing, employment, justice, and nearly every other aspect of daily life.

African American men faced particularly harsh discrimination, especially when it came to work, which often resulted in feelings of helplessness because they weren't able to provide for their families. That led to stress on marriages, and too often, that stress led to separation. The Moynihan Report noted that a disproportionately high number of Black households were headed by women in the 1960s. The reasons why so many Black men were not living at home are complex, and the report doesn't offer satisfactory analysis as to why. But the combined effects on Black men of widespread societal racism, stunted economic opportunities, and a sense of hopelessness in being able to provide for their families led to widespread alienation. And given that we're only a couple of generations on from the Jim Crow era, it's not at all surprising that these challenges have persisted. The impact of this deep-seated, systemic racism on Black families continues to devastate entire communities. One scholar, Dr. Joy DeGruy, calls this "Post Traumatic Slave Syndrome."[12]

"Vacant esteem. Ever present anger. Racist socialization. The effects of almost four centuries of legalized abuse, programmed enslavement and institutionalized oppression can be seen today," Dr. DeGruy writes in her book, *Post Traumatic Slave Syndrome: America's Legacy of Enduring Injury and Healing*. "Centuries of slavery and oppression and the resulting Post Traumatic Slave Syndrome have impacted the lives of many, many African Americans."

She continues, "Added to this condition is a belief (real or imagined) that the benefits of the society in which they live are not accessible to them."[13]

The researcher Jahdziah St. Julien, writing in 2021 for the foundation New America, put it clearly: "The 'absent Black father' myth rests upon the false assumptions that Black fathers simply value parenting less than other fathers and that individual choices, rather than structural and systemic racism, explain why some Black fathers may have difficulty engaging in the lives of their children."[14]

The report notes that when it comes to attitudes toward fatherhood, "Black fathers and white fathers have similar values around caring for their children." Both sets of fathers agreed on the value and need of things like showing love and affection, serving as an authority figure, and providing financial support. (Black dads, however, said that feeding, dressing, and caring for a child was important at higher rates than white dads.)[15]

Simply put, Black dads want to be involved in their kids' lives. But sometimes, societal challenges, especially racism, present too many roadblocks.

It might look different today than in the nineteenth century, but racially driven obstacles are still present, because of disproportionate rates of incarceration, lower access to medical care and mental health services, and sometimes even racist discrimination in social welfare services that quickly villainize and label Black dads as angry or threatening. Thankfully, most Americans understand this reality, even if there sometimes seems to be little agreement about how to address it.

According to a 2019 Pew Research Center study, 63 percent of Americans said that "the legacy of slavery affects the position of Black people in American society today" either "a great deal" or "a fair amount."[16] There's less agreement, however, about whether we've done enough as a society to make up for these lingering effects.

Empowering fathers of color is a specifically anti-racist activity for us at Fathers' UpLift, fighting damaging lies and practices that society has forced onto Black families for centuries. Empowering fathers of color, and subsequently their families, is our part in empowering communities.

There's no shortage of hot takes about what society casually and recklessly calls "absent fathers." One post, published by Fox News, put it bluntly, scolding men who aren't present in the lives of their children—but it didn't engage any of those men to ask why they were absent or if they would like help in trying to reconnect with their kids.[17] This isn't surprising. The voices of the fathers themselves are rarely heard in the discourse around absent dads.

But through my life and my work, I've learned firsthand about the obstacles dads face when they want to reconnect with their kids. Sometimes, there are legal issues, perhaps resulting from an acrimonious relationship with the child's mother. Other times, geographic distance might make being present a challenge. Or maybe so many years have gone by, it's simply impossible to locate where a child lives or know how to contact them.

But there's almost always one constant that comes up in my conversations with men who want to reestablish a relationship with their child: hope. No matter if they've been away for a few months or many years, taking the first step, which is usually a phone call, can feel virtually impossible. Despite the many challenges, I've seen many times how hope has a habit of hanging on. Take George, for example.

I worked with George for nearly a year, as he desperately sought to reestablish a relationship with his daughter, who lived in another state. George had experienced a falling-out with his daughter's mother and was absent not because he didn't care, but because of a three-year legal battle that kept him away. On top of that, he was undergoing intense medical challenges that kept him in the hospital and unable to reach out.

After a particularly harrowing health scare—he actually had prepared for death, but ended up bouncing back—I was able to be with George when he finally reconnected with his daughter. I called him and asked how he felt.

"Charles, hope never left," he told me.

We'll get back to George's story a little later.

But it's important to note that it takes more than hope to reunite an absent dad with his kids. Reappearing in a child's life after months or years of not being present comes with mental and emotional challenges. Absence is a process, growing day by day, and with it, immense shame and guilt for the dad, and anger and resentment for the child. It often takes intense emotional work to overcome those feelings. And not everybody has access to the resources that can help, especially men from marginalized Black and Hispanic communities, who have historically been unable to access essential mental health care.

Mental health is a broad concept that includes different forms of well-being that pertain to one's overall health. Specifically, mental health is a combination of psychological, social, and emotional well-being. An individual's mental health influences how they behave and navigate life's daily stressors. It's at the root of how we manage the stress in our lives and the nature of the decisions we make. Yet we also know that Black Americans, especially men, don't have the access they need to essential mental health services. Economic barriers, shame and stigma, and a lack of Black mental health providers mean that the individuals most in need of life-saving therapy often can't get it. Even when Black men want help improving their mental health, they often face obstacles accessing it.

It's probable that the vast majority of dads, regardless of their unique set of circumstances, need some kind of help learning how to parent, and our society does not do a good job naming that. The result is too many dads afraid to ask for help, not enough help out there for the demand, and kids who suffer.

When a father wants to reconnect with his kids, sometimes the challenges are too great for him to work through on his own, and he simply gives up. But that doesn't mean he's stopped loving his child, even if he isn't equipped with the emotional tools to express that love. He often wants to connect, but he grows frustrated by a series of sometimes small, and other times seemingly intractably large, events that prevent him from taking that first step. I've seen this scenario play out many times, including from Sean, who you met at the beginning of the book.

The first time I met Sean, he was holding a disposable bag in one hand, filled with all his belongings, and a band of black plastic in the other. He had just been released from prison, and he needed a place to charge his ankle monitor. So I showed him to a room, down the hall from my office, where he plugged in the device. We started talking about the reason he was here: his desire to reconnect with his son. It was immediately clear that Sean felt what so many other men in his position feel every day: dread.

When Sean was growing up, he didn't have many expectations for his father, who wasn't around much. His dad's life had been difficult, and that he wasn't a great dad wasn't a surprise given all he had faced as a young man. In many ways, that meant Sean had no experience about what it takes to be a good dad, either. But somehow, he held strong convictions in terms of fatherhood and the responsibilities that came with it. It took two people to make a baby, he reasoned, so fathers need to make an effort to be present in the lives of their children. Sometimes, that means doing what is difficult. It means taming your own ego.

Sean knew firsthand the consequences of making mistakes, poor choices that even lead to separation from your children. It's up to the father to make things right. First, own up to your mistakes. Then, pick up the phone. But that's easier said than done. Especially when the lure of despair is so strong.

Sean recalled the anger he felt as he reflected on the number of days he had been away from his children. Like many men, Sean had not been taught to process his emotions in healthy ways. Instead, he had internalized traits that are now commonly referred to as characteristics of "toxic masculinity," such as a refusal to show emotions, the debilitating need to provide material largesse for one's family, the impulse to be all things for all people. For someone in Sean's position—in jail, stripped of his liberty, and unable to provide—the effects were devastating. He wanted to reach out to his kids, but he needed help. And that meant putting aside his own ego.

Society tells young men that asking for help is somehow emasculating, that real men can do it all on their own. Luckily, Sean was able to see that wasn't true for him, and he was able to reach out for assistance. Once he had that help, Sean was adamant that it was his responsibility to reach out to his children, not the other way around.

Put some verbs in your sentences, throw that mountain off your chest, and pick that phone up, Sean recalled telling himself.

He knew that reaching out didn't guarantee success. His children might be angry with him, wondering why he hadn't reached out sooner. They might feel like Sean had messed up too many times, and perhaps they would reject his attempt to be present in their lives.

The worst-case scenario is "I do not want to talk to you," Sean thought.

But he had to try. He had to confront the reality that his children might not want to speak to him, which weighed heavily on him. He compared it to feeling like he was trapped under a mountain of anxiety.

You have to slam that mountain off your chest and commit to action to reestablish the relationship, he told himself.

The moment had arrived. Sean had been out of prison for a few days. And now he was ready for something he had steeled himself to do for years. It was time to reconnect with his son. The room was silent, and the phone sat idle on a desk. He waited anxiously by the doorway for me to open the door and signal him to come over.

"Charles, I haven't spoken to my kids in years," he told me, his hands damp and fidgety.

"It's okay," I told him. "I'll sit with you while you make the call."

Sean grabbed a wrinkled piece of paper with a number written on it and picked up the phone. His hand seemed stuck, unable to dial. A minute passed. Then another. I stayed seated with Sean, quietly, hoping my presence would let him know that he wasn't alone, that I had his back. Several more minutes passed. But finally, he took a deep breath and dialed the number.

"Hello?" a voice answered.

"Is Tony there?" Sean asked.

"This is him."

"This is your father."

Sean continued to work with us at Fathers' UpLift in the weeks and months following that phone call. Any one of the many challenges he faced could have easily derailed anyone's journey. Following time in jail, he needed an affordable place to live, a seemingly impossible task in the booming Boston market. Then there was the issue of employment, which is never easy for anyone who is trying to put his life back together. On top of that, Sean was dealing with ongoing health issues that included extreme back pain. Taken together, his situation seemed almost hopeless. But with our help, Sean stuck with it, slow step by slow step. We helped him secure an apartment. He started a construction business. Got his health in check. And then, perhaps most important, he mustered up the courage for a trip with me to Boston Children's Museum, where he spent time with his son and grandkids.

There are many memorable scenes from that day, including Sean hugging his son and high-fiving his granddaughters. But there is one particular image that I'll never forget. We were standing inside, with all the bright and noisy activity of a children's museum competing for our attention. But at one moment, I fixated on the group of three men standing in front of me. Sean was wearing a white shirt and a yellow tie. His arm was around his son. Next to him stood his grandson. In some ways, it was an unremarkable scene. There were parents and kids all around us, some of them surely taking the otherwise mundane afternoon outing for granted. But something else was happening here.

Three generations of men stood together, reconnected. The pain and regret hadn't been simply erased, at least not yet. That diminishment will take time. But I saw in their faces the possibility of a better future, a possibility due to Sean putting in the work. Getting his life on track, overcoming the impostor syndrome that had engulfed his sense of confidence. And he forgave himself. For the first time in a long time, Sean felt like he could show up and be the kind of dad he wished he had been all along.

Lesson: Remain aware of what you assume about your students, as you can miss a piece of the puzzle that could be transformative for them. The things we assume to be easy are often more complex than we realize. Showing compassion, embracing simplicity, and seeking understanding can truly make a world of difference.

5. WHAT DOES FATHERHOOD MEAN TO YOU?

Fatherhood is a term that has layers of meanings, and the way a man interprets this word can affect not only his life but his child's as well. For me, the most important part of being a father is showing up. In some ways, that's even more important than biological relations, because I've had men in my life show up to support me who weren't my father. But they showed up when I needed them. I place such importance on showing up because I see my own children light up when I'm with them and because my own father simply wasn't around very much when I was a kid. Those absences created a cycle that was difficult to escape, and by the time I was a teenager, it felt like it was too late. I remember one moment in particular when my father showed up, but not in a way that felt supportive or even genuine to me.

When my mom told me that my dad would be at my high school graduation, I didn't have much to say. After all, I hadn't seen him in five or six years, and aside from an occasional "How are you?" uttered quickly to me on the phone, we didn't have much of a relationship. Even those calls were more upsetting than uplifting. I remember on more than one occasion lying down, listening to Momma talk to my father. Our house was in darkness, and I'm not sure if she knew I could hear both ends of the conversation.

"Charles, can you help me turn my lights on?" she'd ask. "Your son and I have no money."

"I don't have it now," he said. "I can't help!"

Whenever I'd push back, my mother shut down the conversation. Denouncing my father and his misdeeds, pointing out to her that he never visited her in the hospital after a seizure, that didn't work. We'd end up fighting, and Momma would end up waiting by the phone for Dad's next call anyway. It all felt so futile.

Memories of those calls and the fights fueled the rage within me, so when Mom promised he'd be at Riverdale High to watch me walk across the stage and accept my diploma, I didn't feel much at all.

At least that's what I thought.

Graduation was an especially meaningful moment for me. It hadn't been an easy road. I'd struggled with classes, and even though I was captain of my football team and a star athlete, getting into college had been particularly difficult. My coaches weren't eager to help, and it took the tenacity of my mom and her friends from church to get me on the right track.

Now that the high school journey was complete, and I knew I'd be off to college in the fall, I wanted to celebrate my way.

When commencement finished, I tossed my cap into the air and looked around the football field to find Mom. When I spotted her, I saw she wasn't alone. Sure enough, my dad had actually shown up. No one was more surprised than me. I suppose I could have felt relief that he hadn't let down my mom, who was clearly happy that her son's father was present for an important milestone. Or maybe I should have felt angry, because my father's presence once again took my mom's focus off me on what was supposed to be my special day. But standing there on the field that night, I wanted nothing more than to get away.

"We'd like to take you to dinner to celebrate," my mom told me.

This would have been a rare occurrence for the three of us to spend time together, in public, socializing like a normal family. But there was nothing normal about any of this. There had been countless nights over the past eighteen years when my dad could have taken me to dinner. Tonight was not an ordinary night, and I wasn't going to spend it with a man who had been so absent for so long.

"I'm going out with Ant," I told Mom.

I can't remember if she looked hurt. I'm guessing that she wasn't surprised, and perhaps even a little relieved. She probably wasn't looking forward to the awkwardness, either, and though I wasn't rude or disrespectful to my father, I think Mom realized I didn't want much to do with him. Plus, with my deciding to hang out with my cousin, she'd probably get to spend more time with him one-on-one, which suited her just fine.

My cousin Anthony had been my support all through high school. He was more of a dad to me than my father, and I wanted to spend the evening with him. He had planned a night out in Buckhead, the clubby Atlanta neighborhood where we'd be sure to have a good time zipping up and down the main strip. My life at that point had been more or less confined to home, church, and football practice. Even though we didn't live far from Atlanta, the city might as well have been another world.

Ant had organized the whole night, and my other cousins had all agreed to celebrate. That sounded like a lot more fun than a stilted dinner with my mom and a man who considered me to be a shameful secret.

Looking back, I'm surprised I didn't feel more torn on my graduation night. For so long, I had dreamed of being able to spend more time with my father. And there he was, open to having a meal with me and my mom. But he had been gone so long, those dreams had evaporated. Ant had shown up, and I was going to celebrate beginning the next phase of my life with him.

Being present is a choice men make when it comes to how they father their children. But that doesn't mean it's a choice that they have full control over. It's easy to look at a father who isn't present and think, *That's awful he's choosing not to be with his kids.* And maybe it is awful. Sometimes men make selfish decisions. But it's also important to remember that a choice is often not as simple as picking one option over another. Especially not something as complicated as parenting.

In his work, the researcher, psychiatrist, and author Bruce Perry emphasizes how childhood stress creates mental health challenges later on. One study found a relationship between early-life stress, sometimes related to severe adversity, and developmental challenges as early as two months old. Perry's findings point to the importance of understanding how a person's early experiences affect development throughout their life.[18]

To put it another way, it's essential to understand how adverse childhood experiences affect the way we show up, or don't, as parents. Just because something traumatic happened a long time ago doesn't mean it has no impact on the decisions we make today. Time alone doesn't necessarily heal all wounds. As a dad, I'm still learning how important it is for me to remember that my own father's absence during my childhood affects how I parent my two children.

Several years ago, the health care company Kaiser Permanente undertook a longitudinal study after clinicians noted that many of their patients had suffered from historical sexual abuse. The goal of the study, which consisted of interviews with 17,000 people living in Southern California in the 1990s, was to explore the impact that adverse childhood experiences had on a person's health and well-being later in life.

Researchers looked at various adverse childhood experiences and broke them down into three categories. First, there was abuse, including emotional, physical, or sexual. Household challenges came next, and encompassed everything from violence to substance abuse to parental separation. Finally, they looked at childhood neglect, whether emotional or physical. The study underwent some changes over the years, but the results remained more or less consistent. Children who suffered negative experiences faced many obstacles as they grew into adulthood, including physical and mental health challenges, propensity toward risky behaviors, disruptions in development, and overall negative health consequences.[19]

Far too often, the men I work with at Fathers' UpLift are unaware of the powerful relationship between what they endured as children and the choices they make today. Whether that trauma prompts men to make decisions that negatively affect their own health, or prevents them from being present in the lives of their loved ones, I do my best to help these men at least better understand the circumstances shaping their lives.

Take a study from 2004 that appeared in the *Journal of Affective Disorders*. Researchers found that children who experienced childhood emotional abuse had strong associations with depressive symptoms into adulthood. These findings reaffirmed earlier research that highlighted the detrimental impact of emotional or psychological abuse on mental health.[20]

We know that emotional abuse is often intertwined with other forms of abuse, intensifying its consequences. Similarly, adverse childhood experiences are linked to an increased risk of alcohol abuse in later years. Those abusive experiences often significantly increase the risk of drinking profusely, self-reported alcoholism, and even marrying another alcoholic.[21]

I'm not pointing out this research to give men an excuse for the negative decisions they might make later in life, especially around how they interact with their children. Instead, I'm hoping to show that understanding how childhood trauma affects adulthood is productive when it comes to helping men make good decisions. Men often need assistance in healing from their trauma, and society often offers little in terms of understanding or encouragement.

I have worked with hundreds of men over the years, and this theme appears again and again. Men are frequently discouraged from taking their childhood trauma seriously, and as a result, they are powerless to understand how their present-day decisions are shaped by that trauma.

A couple of academic theories have migrated their way into the popular imagination in recent years, and while both add valuable insight into debates about race and gender, neither has been fully effective in bringing about healing to the cohort of men we work with at Fathers' UpLift.

Opposition to the success of the civil rights movement birthed a popular theory we refer to today as Critical Race Theory, which aims to expose the inequities facing people of color. Critical Race Theory sheds light on the continued presence of racism and oppression and how that contributes to the disparities people of color experience. But it doesn't necessarily home in on the wounds that racism produces in the lives of those that experience it, especially Black fathers. The theory primarily exposes the external manifestations of these wounds, such as unfair treatment, but it doesn't address the internal effects, including dislike for one's skin tone, depression, and other internal conflicts. The unseen wounds, like the discomfort a Black person may feel when encountering a police officer, remained unaddressed for a long time. People of color in certain areas may even question their sense of belonging despite it being a safe space for them.

Another theory, dubbed hegemonic masculinity, describes a system that prioritizes men, and a certain understanding of maleness, which results in systems and cultures that exclude women, and those who exhibit nondominant forms of masculinity, from holding power. Gender Studies specialists who explore hegemonic masculinity presuppose that our institutions, including the state, the courts, and even the social safety net, are governed with a narrow view of what it means to be masculine. This reality, they argue, negatively affects those who do not neatly fit into this mold.

As a man and a therapist, I find that many elements of this narrative resonate deeply with my experiences. However, it's crucial to recognize that hegemonic masculinity casts a long shadow, particularly over men of color—both young and old—who are profoundly affected by the interwoven systems of racism, oppression, and residual trauma. This issue is rooted in a culture that shapes our expectations of masculinity. We demand that men embody an often unattainable ideal—strong, stoic, and invulnerable. When they inevitably falter or fail to meet these expectations, we don't extend compassion; instead, we crush them under the weight of our criticism.

Consider our society's adoration for athletes, those extraordinary few who perform physical feats at elite levels. We celebrate their achievements, yet at the same time, we mercilessly shame those who don't excel. This culture of comparison fosters a toxic environment where success is all we accept, leaving little room for vulnerability or growth. We instill this same dynamic in our young men in every area of life, teaching them the notion that they must be tough and always win. We then forbid them from shedding tears even when doing so can be a vital act of healing. We perpetuate harmful stereotypes that dictate how they should express emotion, often leading to detrimental consequences when they suppress what they feel. The message is painfully clear: In our society, winning above all else becomes the ultimate priority.

At Fathers' UpLift, we focus on supporting each person we serve by understanding the multiple ways in which they understand that masculinity contributes to their self-understanding, their setbacks, and their accomplishments. I realized pretty quickly that we needed a more comprehensive and holistic lens through which to view the challenges facing the men we serve. I was able to draw on my research on self-parenting and the inner child to create a method of exploring how external forces shape a man's worldview, including around fatherhood.

In the joining together of racism, oppression, trauma, and hegemonic masculinity, each contributes to what I call the Internal Masculinity Conflict. The IMC sheds light on the internal parental struggle that occurs between a man and himself. It's an ongoing, internal battle, which ensues when a conflict arises between a man's ideal image of what it means to be a father, the image of the kind of father he wants to be, and the father he believes society expects him to be.

This internal battle begins when a man is convinced that external forces or actors are questioning his role as father, whether it be relatives, the mother of his child, or even systems such as child welfare or the courts. This subsequently leads to the father questioning his capacity to be a good dad to his children, however he's defined "good" for himself. This self-questioning of his ability to fulfill the role eventually translates into feelings of worthlessness, shame, sadness, or anger. These emotions vary based on the nature and origin of the father's internal conflict.

Put another way, the Internal Masculinity Conflict is a set of conflicting emotions and decisions facing men, especially men who struggle to be mentally and physically present in their children's lives.

Responses to the IMC are varied, but I've seen trends and believe that they often manifest in three categories: Injured Provider, Provoked Fear, and Avoidant Vulnerable.

INJURED PROVIDER

A father's struggle to meet his family's financial and emotional needs, as perceived through societal expectations, often creates an injured provider. This reality arises when a father feels unable to fulfill the traditional role of provider, leading to a fight-or-flight response. He may seek ways to meet the ideal provider's expectations, in healthy or unhealthy ways, or he may distance himself from his children or spouse, reinforcing his perceived failure to support his family financially.

PROVOKED FEAR

Fathers who fear repeating the harmful patterns foisted on them by their parental figures fall into the category of provoked fear. These fathers are often anxious about potentially adopting the exact traits that harmed them during their childhood. These men might distance themselves from their children, believing that their absence is ultimately better for their family's well-being. They may be partly motivated to adopt this model of fatherhood because they are striving for unattainable perfection as dads and husbands in order to protect their loved ones. This behavior reflects their past experiences of harsh treatment, leading men to go to extreme lengths to prevent causing harm, even if this appears irrational to others.

AVOIDANT VULNERABLE

Fathers sometimes suppress their emotions to avoid being perceived as weak. These fathers may not be aware of their emotional struggles and refrain from expressing their feelings. The fear of appearing vulnerable leads them to avoid situations that might prompt emotional responses, such as displaying affection. This avoidance stems from a belief that showing emotion is a sign of weakness, which could be misconstrued as selfishness or insensitivity.

None of these external challenges exist in isolation. Even as the pressures of fatherhood mount, the men I counsel still struggle with internal challenges. Especially in environments where racism, oppression, and trauma intersect, the choices fathers make might be seen by themselves as rational and necessary for survival, even if those on the outside see them as irrational or even illegal.

I recall an incident that illustrates these societal pressures all too well. One day, following a therapy session, a father was harassed outside my office. The police officer showed no regard for the fact that I was his therapist. Instead, he sought to instill fear in this dad, based solely on the assumption that he resembled someone from the officer's past, where previous conflict set the stage for toxic interactions.

At that moment, I decided to intervene, to advocate for the father, only to discover the flip side of the system when detectives called me in for interrogation. Rather than holding the officer accountable or seeking ways to rectify the situation, the focus shifted to scrutinizing the man already battling posttraumatic stress disorder, a daunting challenge he had worked tirelessly to overcome. That experience led the dad once again to question the perception of himself, his masculinity, and, in turn, his ability to be a father.

So what can a man do when experiences from his past continue to shape his present—beyond just acknowledging that reality, an important first step? One theory from child psychologist Selma Fraiberg offers some helpful ideas that I've incorporated into my own work.

In her 1974 lecture to the Boston Psychoanalytic Society and Institute, entitled "Ghosts in the Nursery," Fraiberg explained how parents sometimes unknowingly reenact their own early experiences of helplessness and fear with their children. This in turn perpetuates child maltreatment, continuing to create trauma across generations. At the same time, Fraiberg said, a parent can help a child secure a sense of self-worth when the child feels deeply understood, accepted, and loved.[22]

I've thought a lot about all this research, and I use an approach with the men with whom I work that urges them to recognize the positive influences—or "angels," as I call them—who exist in their lives. This doesn't mean that we stop recognizing and seeking to understand past trauma, but it gives us a chance to look at positive influences at the same time.

A father repeating his past struggles with his own children isn't ideal, but it's human and it happens. But if a man remains aware of his angels, he may give himself permission to display empathy despite the presence of triggers. This isn't always easy, but the ability to exercise empathy, over maltreatment, comes with self-introspection and ongoing awareness.

Like anyone else, the men I counsel make sense of their worlds through their own experiences. Take the story of Marcus, a dad I worked with who often traveled mentally back to his childhood.

As a child, Marcus had a close relationship with his mother, a dedicated nurse whom he holds up as a role model. But when Marcus and his mother moved to Florida, a chance for a new beginning, Marcus's life took a turn. His stepfather, Derek, seemed cool at first, but there was something frightening about him Marcus couldn't quite place.

One night, for example, Marcus's mom told him and his sister that they could stay up late, a rare treat. But when Marcus's stepfather came into their room and demanded he and his sister go to sleep, the atmosphere became tense. Marcus explained that his mom had said he and his sister could stay up late. This angered Derek, who grabbed an extension cord. He held it menacingly and stood there, staring down the two children. On that night, Derek didn't strike Marcus or his sister, but a sense of fear overtook the home. And it was a preview of what was to come.

The threat of abuse was actualized, and Marcus went on to bear both mental and physical scars from his stepfather's beatings. Too ashamed to tell anyone, he carried that pain into his adulthood. As he prepared to become a father, he worried how this unresolved trauma would affect his relationship with his daughter. He battled addiction and anger issues, the result of his inner child still being scared of his stepfather's abuse.

Through intensive counseling and coaching, Marcus began to heal, and one important component of that journey was his ability to focus on his angels, including his mother and his grandparents. Spending time with them, the adults who loved him and treated him kindly, had provided a respite from his otherwise chaotic childhood. By focusing on these angels, Marcus has been able to reclaim his life and take it back from the ghosts that continued to haunt him long after his stepfather was no longer in his life.

Remembering to seek out the hidden angels in our lives requires patience and perseverance. Even in the heat of adversity, most individuals still cling to glimmers of hope that their circumstances can improve and that a brighter future is within reach. Negative memories can cloud that hope, but they might not extinguish it entirely. The resilient and tenacious human spirit possesses an innate drive to fight against despair, even when that fight feels buried beneath layers of pain and doubt. Amid the chaos of negative recollections, moments of clarity can ignite change, illuminating paths toward acceptance and growth. Each small victory—a shared laugh, a comforting word, or a fleeting moment of joy—can serve as a reminder that the possibility of light always exists, even in the darkest of times.

By acknowledging and embracing these fragments of hope, we can cultivate the strength needed to confront our pasts and forge ahead into a future defined not by our struggles but by our resilience. The process may be extended and fraught with challenges. Still, every attempt to uncover those angels offers the promise of renewal, allowing us to reclaim the narrative of our lives and rewrite it with purpose and grace.

Inevitably, there are moments in a father's life when other adults, or sometimes even his own children, come to symbolize harmful moments from his past. This often leads to unpleasant bouts of anger and hate, sometimes the products of lingering, unresolved childhood traumas. These moments are natural and even insightful. I try to help men see them as opportunities for growth, so they can imagine how they can turn to their angels for reminders of their importance and as examples to emulate. Mirroring these giants from their pasts, or in other words, "angels in the nursery," can guide these men to be present as the best version of themselves.

No one is immune to the reality that past experiences shape how we live today. In my life, when I am in different or unknown places, I constantly remind myself that I belong. My past has made it difficult to feel at ease in different environments simply because of the memory of the day my father left my life. This isn't surprising to me, as I've spent significant time trying to find a place where I belong—where I could feel at home amid the chaos. I haven't always succeeded, and it's been unfair to people who have had to deal with how I've expressed my own abandonment issues. I don't wish that kind of treatment and coldness on anyone. But when our trauma is at the steering wheel, we have no other choice but to be the passenger. We can try to be a backseat driver, but we simply aren't in control. And unfortunately, the reality of our past experiences, if not dealt with, frequently leads to generational trauma.

Choosing to be nurturing, or choosing to be abusive, as much as either is a freely made choice, often is a result of our life experiences. Sometimes, though, we don't even realize that the choices we're making are the result of past experiences, good or bad. These are called *blind choices*. The patterns of our choices become habits. But we can shift away from unhealthy habits. This shift occurs when our choices align with the memories of our angels. When the angels become our center of intention, instead of the harmful effects of our past experiences, we can begin to make the kinds of choices we know deep down we want to make.

Blind choices often result in acting out of character. Have you ever gotten into a nasty argument, where you were tempted to say or do something you would have never wanted to see yourself say or do? In my own life, I've had moments where I would automatically think that I was unworthy of a person's love and distance myself. This has occurred with Samantha and me. I almost lost her because I didn't think I was good enough for her. When you are convinced that you are unworthy, you will do anything to live up to the label you have placed on your life. The lingering effects of trauma do not go away just because you grow older. That temptation is a blind choice. I didn't understand it in the heat of the moment, but my past experiences were tempting me to act in a way that was not in accord with who I imagine myself to be.

On the other hand, *conscious choices* are made when someone is fully aware. A person is determined that he or she will make a certain choice and can share the rationale behind that choice, even when it might not make sense to others.

Past experiences shape present-day decisions, so I've found it helpful in my own life, and in my work at Fathers' UpLift, to focus on the angels rather than the ghosts. I've developed a few tricks that help me keep my angels close.

It might sound silly, but I actually make it a practice to remember the names of my angels. I try to recall when they entered my life and what they did for me that made me feel loved and safe. Then, I try to think of two or three words that describe the difference each of them made in my life.

Keeping pictures of my angels nearby helps me visualize them, and wearing jewelry or clothing that belonged to my angels prompts me to envision them during particularly difficult times. I keep trinkets that remind me of them, and I sometimes make it a point to cook a meal for my family that I remember eating with my angels. These meals are about more than the food. They are opportunities to create new memories, tying current experiences to pleasant times from my past.

Sometimes I'll visit places that remind me of quality time spent with my angels. When I can, I look at photos or watch videos featuring my angels, or if I don't have access to photos or videos, I'll listen to music or put on movies that connect me to them. Each of these rituals are ways to keep my angels close, especially during moments when I could use a helping hand in confronting the daily challenges of life. Let me tell you about one of my angels.

I was recently on vacation with my family in Puerto Rico, creating new memories for us that I hope our children will carry fondly throughout their lives. We were visiting an organization with our friend Rob, a social entrepreneur from Oakland, California, and dad to a beautiful young girl. I call Rob a "present keeper" because of his ability to get folks around him to live in the present. He's someone I've come to see as a father figure in my own life. While in Puerto Rico, as I stared in awe at the natural beauty, Rob noticed a change in my demeanor.

"Charles, I am here with you at this moment," he told me. "It's beautiful seeing you experience this for the first time." Rob is not my biological father, but at that moment, he was a dad with me, present in the moment. His observation was another reminder of the power of being present.

Later on, as I was staring out over an inlet, where the river meets the beach, I heard in the depths of my heart a soft, gentle voice.

"Don't ever forget them," the voice said.

I took that as a reminder to myself to remember the father figures in my life, my angels, who have been there for me. Especially the father figures who, because I was so focused at the time on the deficits in my life, took me a while to acknowledge as father figures. The profound presence of the fathers in my life transformed me even when I could not see them. I see now that God uses the fathers in our lives to remind us of His presence.

That message, "Don't forget them," was also a prompt, I believe, for me to remind society more broadly to acknowledge the fathers and father figures who show up, who are present for their children, biological and otherwise. To be present is to remember, to remember those who have loved us into being and those who need our love. Put another way, that moment of contemplation provided me another opportunity to recall my angels.

It's taken me time and practice, but I can confidently say today that in moments of crisis, I can actually envision my angels and lean on them as I make a decision about my life. When my angel says that I matter, I remember that I matter. And that helps me make decisions that tell those I love, those I work with, that they matter, too.

My interactions with my angels live on, even as I get older. If research shows that negative past experiences haunt people for years, then it makes sense that positive past experiences shape us, too. Those memories of how my angels made me feel have the same effects today as they did when I experienced it in the moment, alive and in the flesh. Their presence nurtures me, warmly embracing my soul when I feel shame, anger, or grief. Their presence also reminds me of my worth, that someone truly cares about me in the flesh and spirit. I know now that I need to remember my angels during this journey. My sanity and the lasting image of my own presence as an angel in the lives of other people depend on it.

For others who find that they feel burdened by their pasts, I encourage them to reconsider their stories, and to re-translate them. Like Marcus, whose memories from his childhood seemed to be filled only with the ghosts of his stepfather's abuse. Turning his attention to his angels changed his life. By focusing instead on moments when he felt safe and protected, like cruising down the highway with his mom in her convertible, Marcus reframed his life for himself. This gave him the ability to reimagine his future. This kind of reimagining is possible for each of us, and it is a critical part of the healing journey.

Lesson: There are always people who show us joy when we think of them. Who are those people for the "students" in our lives? Where are the angels in the "classrooms"? Every opportunity to remind ourselves of an angel is a moment that never gets old. Knowing the nature of conflict and the angels that love us can lighten any load.

6. SHOWING UP

One of the most important lessons we try to impart to the men we work with is the importance of showing up. I remember working with one father who told me that he didn't feel like he could be present to his kids in a meaningful way because he lacked the money to buy them what he felt they deserved. It was easier for him simply to not be around often than to confront the reality that he couldn't provide in the way he wanted. His idea of masculinity was being a provider. But showing up often costs nothing, and it can go a long way. I know this from my own life.

Following high school, I eventually enrolled at Bethune-Cookman University, an HBCU in Daytona Beach, Florida, about six hours south of where we lived in Georgia. I was ready for a fresh start, but one hurdle remained.

After tallying up the grants, loans, and scholarship money, I still owed Cookman $3,000 for the first year, which was due before I would be allowed to begin classes. Stress over money was a constant in my life, and this time, feeling like my future was on the line, it made me sick. I was exhausted. I wasn't eating well. I even ended up in the hospital because of complications arising from malnutrition. My momma saw the toll that the stress was taking on me, both mentally and physically. As she always did, she tried to make things better.

Sensing what was at stake, she got in the car and drove several hours to Valdosta to see my father. The journey by herself was risky, because a seizure could happen at any time. That could make driving long distances particularly dangerous.

But Mom arrived safely and told my father about my health issues and explained that I needed to find $3,000 in order to enroll at Cookman. My father still hadn't been very involved in my life, but Momma hoped that perhaps he might see my desire to take classes as an opportunity to step up for me.

The financial aid office had told Mom that the best way to cover the shortfall was to take out a loan, which, for a young man with little credit history, meant finding someone to cosign on my behalf. Momma would not have hesitated, but she faced financial obstacles related to her health and losing much of her retirement in the Great Recession. Her credit made it unlikely that she would be able to secure the loan for me. She explained all this to my father.

"I told him I would ask you," she said. "He really wants to attend."

My father paused for a moment.

"Yeah, I'll do it," he said. "Let me know when you get down there."

When Momma told me the news, I was overjoyed. Though still recovering from malnutrition, I felt alive and started to imagine a future in which things finally seemed back on track. Though I would have to wait until the start of the spring semester to enroll at Cookman, I could already feel the pride welling up inside me.

Several weeks later, Momma and I hit the road, headed for Daytona Beach.

"Momma," I said during the drive, "this is unbelievable. I'm surprised that Dad is going to cosign the loan for me. Talk about a change in him. Wow."

My mother shared in my excitement, even if her tone was more tempered.

"Your dad said he would take care of it," she said. "We'll see."

We arrived on campus and walked to the financial aid office. Looking around, I noticed the sense of campus pride that seemed to be everywhere, with maroon-and-gold in every sight line. The paperwork had been processed, and we were good to go. All we needed was for my father to provide his financial information, sign a couple of forms, and the loan would be in the works. I would proudly take my seat at Cookman.

Momma reached into her purse, found her cellphone, and called my father. The financial aid officer and I sat quietly as Momma talked to my father.

"Charles, we're in Daytona Beach," she said to my father. "I need your information so they can prepare the forms for you. When you receive them, sign them and return them to the school."

Silence followed.

The hope and joy and excitement that had animated our morning evaporated.

Momma apologized to the financial aid office and rose from her seat. She walked to an enclosed vestibule in the back of the office and continued talking to my father. She wanted privacy but I was desperate to hear the news, any news, and listened intently.

"Charles, we need you," she pleaded. "You told me you would cosign for the remaining balance. We're here, now, in Daytona Beach. Please, Charles."

They went back and forth for thirty minutes. She asked again politely, then firmly, then got heated.

"This is what he wants, Charles," she said. "Your son wants to go here."

My father must have hung up, because I saw my mother furiously dial the phone, wait a few moments, and then yell.

"You hear this phone ringing!" she railed. "Answer the phone. Please."

She tried again. Still no answer.

I looked down at my hands and played with my nails. I was embarrassed. Angry. Most of all, my heart was broken. I didn't want the financial aid officer to see me cry, so I got up and walked around the office. I tried convincing myself that Momma would return with a solution. That short walk back to the chair felt heavy. What would Momma say to make this nightmare go away?

"Ms. McLaren," she said to the administrator, "you can try to run my credit."

A Hail Mary pass, but Momma would try anything to make this right.

As the administrator punched in Momma's information, my stomach churned. It felt like all my hard work hung in the balance. Whatever the computer said would determine my future.

The drive back home was the worst of my life.

The financial aid officer had explained that Momma's credit wasn't sufficient to secure the loan. And without the $3,000 I needed to cover my balance, I couldn't enroll. I was angry at my father, for again failing to show up at a time when I needed him. I saw my future again being determined by circumstances created by other people, individuals who failed to take responsibility. I felt like I had no control over anything, and my mind spun with rage. I was so devastated in my own loss, and tunnel vision took over.

Looking back, I can't imagine the shame and anger and embarrassment Momma felt. She had done her best to help me achieve my dreams—but it hadn't been enough. Her heart, too, must have been broken. And we still had six hours in a car together to let our emotions stew.

When we finally arrived home, I raced upstairs, shut my bedroom door, and let everything I had been feeling that day pour out. My tears wet my pillow, and I oscillated wildly between rage, sadness, disappointment, and confusion. Why hadn't my father signed the papers? What was it about me that repelled him? Was I doing something so wrong that my own father refused to help when I needed him most? It was almost too much to bear.

Over the next few days, reality set in. Hard. Instead of taking classes, playing football, and making friends, I spent my days inside bleak factories and warehouses, working for an hourly wage. My future never seemed less my own than during those many months.

A year later, Momma and I packed the car again and drove the six hours down to Cookman. Again, we parked and walked to the financial aid office. Things felt largely the same. The administrator invited us to take a seat. I was too anxious to relax, so I remained standing. When Ms. McLaren finished typing, she said that the result was the same as last year: I needed to secure a loan of $3,000 before I could enroll in classes.

But this time, my mother had a plan.

A longtime friend of Momma's, a man I called Uncle Larry,

had been present in our lives for as long as I could remember. Tall, slim, and with a honey-brown complexion, Larry lit up any room he entered. The glint in his eye always made me feel good when he was around. He'd buy me candy, take me to parks. Simple things my father should have been doing. But when I was with Uncle Larry, none of that mattered. Feeling like someone, like Larry cared enough about me to spend time with me, made me feel on top of the world.

Momma took her phone from her purse and dialed Larry's number. She stayed in her seat, seemingly confident that she wouldn't need to step away for privacy this time. She spoke confidently, and there was even an edge of excitement in her voice. Were my dreams finally on the verge of realization?

I stood close to Momma, so near that I could hear Larry's voice on the phone.

"Anything I can do to support Charles, I'll do," Larry said.

I am not related to Larry by blood. He has no obligation to support me, never mind cosigning a loan that would put him on the line if I couldn't repay. But he stepped up, even when he could have reasonably said no. My own father may have sidestepped his responsibility to his son, but here was a man who acted as a father figure. I breathed a sigh of relief. The forms were processed. And my future finally seemed my own.

When I look back on my childhood, I realize now that Larry seemed to be there for every major milestone. He attended football games. He saw me off to my prom. He even watched me graduate. Larry cheered me on every step of the way.

"I want to thank you for everything you've done for me," I told him years later, my voice filled with emotion. "I know that

I'm not your biological son, but you've been more of a father to me than I could have ever asked for."

Larry listened quietly, his eyes welling up with tears. I could have stopped there, but something had been nagging at me.

"What made you do it?" I asked.

Larry was still for a moment and seemed to be considering his words before speaking.

"Charles, you've always been my son in my heart," he said. "I may not have contributed to your DNA, but I have contributed to your life, and I will always love you as my own."

Larry filled in some gaps for me. He and my mom had dated on and off, but even when they weren't together, Larry would still do what he could to help me. When I was applying for college, Larry and my mom weren't together. But when Larry heard what was going on, he said he had no choice but to help.

"Your mother came to me, and I knew how smart you are, how driven you are," he said.

My mom had told Larry about the need for a cosigner, and pledged that if I ever defaulted on the loan, she would pay it off for me.

"It was a no-brainer for me," Larry told me. "I knew you were going to make something of your life. Charles, you were a good kid. You ain't never really got in any trouble. You didn't cause your mother any trouble. You didn't do anything wrong, no drinking, no drugs, nothing like that. So, it would have been sad to see somebody with your potential not have the opportunity to fulfill their goals in life."

Larry said that he wouldn't have been able to live with himself if he hadn't stepped up. He wanted to see me have an opportunity to go to school, so he signed the forms. The conversation between Larry and me that day was a powerful testament to the extraordinary love that he had shown me. Though he tried to downplay his good deed, I wouldn't hear it. Through his actions, his sacrifices, and his unwavering support, Larry had proven to me at a pivotal time in my life that men are capable of deep, selfless love. He had stepped up and stood in as a father for a son who did not belong to him, and in doing so, he showed me that love knows no boundaries, limits, or genetic code.

On a hot August afternoon in 2022, I called Larry to share some news: The loan that he had cosigned all those years earlier was finally paid off. It was a celebratory moment and one I wanted to share with the man who had made it possible to begin with.

"Uncle Larry," I said into the phone, "the loan is paid off!"

He was nonplussed. Perhaps he picked up that I felt a bit let down that he didn't share in my excitement?

"Charles," he said, "I never had any doubt you'd pay off the loan!"

We both laughed, and I told him again that I would be forever grateful to the men who gave me a chance, including him.

Larry always loved me like a son. But he rejected that framing, of "loving like a son." I was his son.

Sometimes fathers, especially new dads, are so overwhelmed with everything they need to provide for their children that they can't imagine a way forward. Whether it's money, like in my father's case, emotional support, or even time, sometimes dads feel that because they aren't able to provide, they have no value. They disappear. But just being present is its own kind of providing.

Lesson: Consistently displaying our care, even when difficulties arise, means a lot to the student. Aggressively believing in a student and conveying our beliefs verbally and through our actions could be all they need to get through the difficult moments each time. This requires one thing: showing up.

7. A FATEFUL CALL

Coaching men to pick up the phone to call their children, sometimes for the first time in years, is a regular part of my work. The effort required to get to this point isn't always easy, but the payoff can be rewarding. I've seen it many times. In my own life, however, the roles have often been reversed. I've picked up the phone a few times. And the results haven't always been as encouraging. But making the calls, insisting on communication, has made me aware of the fatherhood lessons that come from making the effort. I remember one call in particular.

"Hello," I said into the phone. "Is Uncle Roy available?"

Those five words set off a course of events that quite literally changed my life.

One Saturday a few years ago, Samantha and I met for lunch in Valdosta, Georgia. Valdosta was about halfway for the two of us, so it was a good meeting spot for our long-distance relationship. Coincidentally, Valdosta also happened to be a place of great importance when it comes to the story of my family.

"Samantha," I said, "my dad's side of the family actually lives here—and I've never met any of them."

At this point in my life, I had recently graduated college, and the pain I felt about my father backtracking on his promise to help me secure a loan had begun to fade. Even though it was a convenient meeting spot for Samantha and me, it was no accident that I was in Valdosta. I had brought something that could help me figure out who I was: the phone number of my father's brother, my uncle Roy.

"I wonder if they'd come and meet me if I called them?" I asked Samantha.

In the idealized version of events I imagined, I would call Uncle Roy, who would be elated to hear from the nephew he never knew. He would then put me in touch with my father's other children, my siblings, plus the rest of my cousins. We would meet up and I would begin the process of creating the strong, tight-knit extended family I had longed for. The plan seemed reasonable, but I had my doubts.

"Maybe I shouldn't," I said in response to my own query. "I'd be opening up something that I don't need to be opening."

Samantha was having none of my self-doubt.

"You should call them," she said matter-of-factly. "That is your family, and you want to meet them."

It was hard to argue with that. Despite my father's best efforts to keep me a secret, they were my family, and I was part of theirs. I did want to meet them, even if the fear of further rejection remained lodged deep in my chest. Despite that, the decision was made. I would reach out to my family.

"Roy's not home," said the woman who answered the phone, his wife, Angeline. He was attending a funeral down in Gainesville, Florida. She didn't know when he'd return.

"Could you let him know that his nephew, Charles Jr., is in town and that I want to see him?" I asked.

Angeline told me that she would relay my message and that Roy would call me when he got home. Looking back, I can't imagine what was going through Angeline's mind. I didn't know if she was aware of my existence or what she felt about my father. Had I opened up a part of her husband's family's history that they all preferred to keep sealed? Or maybe Roy was actually home, and his wife told a white lie so as not to stir up any drama?

After an hour or so and not hearing from Roy, I called back. I had accepted that maybe Roy didn't want to speak to me, so my plan was to ask Angeline for the numbers of my father's two sisters, Patricia and Viola. If Roy wasn't going to be the person to introduce me to my siblings, perhaps these two women might be willing to help.

"Oh, Charles, he's just walking through the door now. Hold on!" Angeline said. I heard her yelling for Roy. "Charles Jr. is on the phone!"

Roy picked up. I held my breath.

When I tell this story, people sometimes ask how I felt. Nervous? Anxious? Scared? Excited? The truth is, I didn't know what to feel. I knew this conversation would be momentous, but I still wasn't sure how it would go. My whole life, I had yearned to know more about my father, my family. And while there had been a few false starts over the years, I knew in my bones that this would be different. I felt all those emotions, but I wasn't able to process them that quickly.

"Charles," he said, "how's everything going with you?"

"Hey, I'm good, Uncle Roy," I said.

The ice broke. I had found a part of my family that could

help make me whole. And the first steps were taken. There was no going back now.

I apologized if the unexpected call was too much for him to take in and, giving him an out, said that if he was busy and couldn't meet, I'd understand. But Roy brushed all that aside.

"Not at all, Charles," he said. "I want to meet you. I'll definitely come and see you."

The hotel where Samantha and I were staying was near where Roy and the other Danielses lived. When the knock on the door finally came, I was shocked to see not only Roy, but also his brother, my uncle Chandler. A seemingly impulsive quest to connect with one uncle resulted in meeting two. I was both nervous and elated.

My uncles filled in gaps in my family history that Momma either didn't tell me or didn't know herself. First, I learned that my paternal grandfather, L. B. Daniels, had founded a church, which he named after his wife, my grandmother Grace. Uncle Roy told me that he was co-pastor of Grace Victory Church, along with his brother, my uncle Buster. Uncle Jimmy, meanwhile, chaired the deacon's board. Preaching, it seemed, was a family trait. Another uncle, Monte, had died from a stroke a few years earlier. I was learning so much about my family, and my emotions were in overdrive.

My grandfather had built a successful church, and my uncles continued his legacy. I felt a sense of pride. At the same time, I was angry that I was just learning about these stories for the first time. And while I was grateful to be in the presence of three of my uncles, I was also sad to learn that the reunion had come too late to meet a fourth.

I was still processing all these revelations when I suddenly blurted out the question that had been driving me for so many years.

"Uncle, how many brothers and sisters do I have?"

It was a deeply personal question. I had grown up an only child, and even though I was fortunate to have deep connections with the many cousins who were present in my life, once I knew that my father had other children, I resented that I had been denied the opportunity to know my brothers and sisters. It took a lot of courage for me to ask this question, which is why their reaction surprised me.

Roy looked at his brother and they began to laugh.

Perhaps sensing my confusion, Roy turned to me.

"Charles, I don't know," he said. "At least a couple. But to tell you the truth, they could be standing in a store next to me and I couldn't even tell you who they were."

My father's secret, that he had fathered children with women other than his wife, was apparently not as secret as he liked to pretend. His brothers were vaguely aware of his situation, even if they didn't know the specifics.

From that conversation, I learned that my father had two other sons for certain, Calvin and Terry. Later conversations with other members of my dad's family revealed that he also had a daughter, June, and another son, Ishmuil. All told, my father had six children with three different women. He had done his best to keep his children apart, evidently afraid of what might happen should they ever cross paths. But we were adults now, and the feeling that we were secrets to be hidden rather than fully alive human beings seeking to understand their origins would no longer suffice.

After we visited for a while, my uncles said they had to get going, so I wrote down my phone number for them. I asked them to stay in touch and if they knew how I might meet my brothers. They go to church sometimes, Roy told me. So perhaps I could meet them there.

The meeting had gone better than expected. That they even showed up was a small miracle. That they were kind and willing to answer my many questions was an added grace.

What I hadn't known during our meeting was that my mother had called my father to let him know of my plans. I don't know how my father reacted to the news—it's certainly easy to imagine him being furious with my mother for giving me his brother's phone number. But regardless of how he felt, the meeting had taken place.

So when I walked my uncles to the hotel lobby, we were all shocked to see my father's car parked out front. He was walking toward us.

"Hey boy," he said, as if seeing me in person, talking to his brothers, was somehow ordinary and unremarkable. "How's everything going?"

That kind of question is a normal query between a father and his adult son. But I hadn't seen my father in years. Here I was in his hometown standing next to three of his brothers. The question didn't capture the weight of the moment. But I didn't make a scene or reply hostilely. There was too much at stake.

"Good as usual," I said. "Just working and saving money so I can go to graduate school."

"You better save because I don't have any," he shot back. "That check I'm getting ain't doing nothing for me."

My uncles laughed. I cringed. Our first meeting in years, and my father immediately assumed I was there to ask him for money. All I really wanted was something he could give me for free: his time.

Despite that awkward joke, my father was charming and funny. He explained that his twenty-seven years working at a chemical plant had seemingly counted for nothing when the company decided to cut costs. They eliminated his position and reassigned him to work on the roof of a train.

"Man, I told them I ain't working on top of nothing. I'm fifty-eight years old, you tryna kill me? From my office to a train. You can fire me!" he recalled.

I laughed at the absurdity. But then got down to business.

"Dad, my uncles told me about Calvin and Terry."

Something snapped in his demeanor. My father's forehead wrinkled with anger.

"Oh yeah?" he said.

His staccato answer ended that line of questioning.

We shifted around uncomfortably and decided to take a group photo. My father grabbed my shoulder, looked me in the eye, and said, "Hurry up and finish school so you can take care of me, you hear?"

My father left first, claiming that he had errands to run. My uncles headed toward their cars. I asked them not to forget about me. They promised they wouldn't.

As I watched my father and his brothers drive away, I said to myself, "I forgive you, Father."

I wanted so badly for that sentiment to be true. By voicing it aloud, I tried to manifest it into existence. The anger, resentment, shame, and fury that had consumed me for my entire life could evaporate if I could make that forgiveness a reality. But it wasn't. I was nowhere near ready to forgive my father.

The next morning, I posted the photo to Facebook. It was the only tangible evidence that I had connected with my father and my uncles, and despite my mixed feelings about the way the meeting ended, I wanted the world to see it. I knew deep down that my father would be upset if he knew I was sharing my news with the wider world, but it was my news to share. I was tired of being the family secret.

When I was a kid, I had heard that my father was married. I'm not sure how that piece of information reached me, but once I knew it, I began imagining what life must be like for his other family. Those visions only added to my anger. But my father's marriage had always been a rumor. Momma certainly wasn't going to confirm any details. But when I connected with my cousin Latanya, who had seen the photo of my father, my uncles, and me, on Facebook, I had the opportunity to learn the truth.

"Latanya, is my father married?" I asked over the phone.

"Yes, he is."

"And do Calvin and Terry have the same mother?"

"Yes, they do."

I couldn't catch my breath. The family life that I had imagined as a child was true. Latanya said that my father was married and that he and his wife raised their children together. Their home was even a gathering place for the extended family. The Danielses had cookouts, went to amusement parks together. They were the tight-knit family I had so desired as a kid.

What Latanya said next stung.

"Your father was always there," she said.

Back home, I told Momma about everything that had transpired down in Valdosta. I told her about Roy and my other uncles, how my father had come to see me. I told her how I had posted the photo to Facebook and how I wanted the world to know about my newfound family. I told her how I had found a cousin because of that photo and how she helped me track down my brothers, Calvin and Terry. And I told her how I planned to meet them.

"Lord Jesus!" she said. "Are you serious?"

With the deluge of information about my father's family

coming at me all at once, I was too busy processing my own emotions to consider how all this news might affect Momma. After all, my father's penchant for keeping secrets meant that Momma didn't know much about his life down in Valdosta. Sure, she was aware that she saw my father only intermittently and she suspected that he was busy with another family. But the details of his life were not for her to know; at least that's how my father evidently felt. Or if she did know about them, she chose not to spend much time dwelling on unpleasant details. At that moment, I sensed how my own journey to meet my family would have ripples into the lives of others I already knew and loved.

I was telling Momma about Calvin, how he was twenty-five years old and lived down in Valdosta. I kept going with some more news I had learned when she stopped me.

"He's two years older than you . . ." she said, her voice trailing off.

My mother hadn't known about Calvin, and this revelation made her sad. And angry. My father had kept his other family a secret. He had young children at home, all while she raised me on my own. It seemed like it just occurred to her at this moment that my father's absence was the other side of the coin, that he was a father to other children.

She composed herself.

"Take that photo off of Facebook. Your father is a private person," she said. "Stop digging."

Even if I had wanted to honor Momma's wish, it was too late. My uncles not only knew about me, but we had all met in person. I had talked to a cousin and my sister on the phone. What difference did a photo make at this point? To stop digging was simply not possible. Plus, I had no desire to stop. I love my momma but her request was too much for me.

I was more determined than ever to meet my family and to unearth my own history.

Church has always played a central role in my life. Back when I was twelve, I was asked to read a poem in church about what fatherhood meant to me. I can still remember the deaconess calling me up to the stage. She introduced me, and the congregation clapped. But I was sweating and could feel everyone's eyes prying into me. Somehow, I had managed to write a poem about fatherhood, even as my own father was never around. In retrospect, the poem lists qualities of a father I could only imagine, qualities my own father seemed incapable of possessing.

"Love, teach, and care," I read. "Those three things are needed in a real man who has the responsibility of a father."

I read on, laying out how a father should act. He should love his wife, treating her like a precious gift. He should love his child, teaching him how to love his neighbor and his God.

"Last but not least," I said, "caring. No matter what happens, a father cares for the wife and child. Caring is what they need, caring for them like God cares for you."

It made sense, given my past, that church would once again be the setting for a defining moment in my life. I decided I would go to the church my grandparents had built, both to see their legacy firsthand and to meet more of my family. Heading to church, I imagined what I would say to my father when I confronted him. I played it over in my head, building up the courage with each reiteration of the pending encounter.

"Hey Charles Sr., you son of a bitch," I imagined myself saying. "What were you thinking? You played my momma.

When she was sick, you did nothing. No visit, no phone call. You're pathetic. In fact, you're selfish."

In this imagined interaction, my father would be so shocked by this dressing down that I would have the time and wherewithal to let everything that had built up over the years spill out. My childhood fears about Momma having a seizure on one of those long drives to meet my father. My loneliness as I sat home alone waiting for her to return. The pain I felt seeing my mother upset and crying when she wouldn't hear from my father. How I had a secret family, who seemed kind and close-knit, who had been kept from me. How my father had let my grandfather die before giving me the chance to meet him.

"You call yourself a man," I imagined saying. "I call you a punk—and I refuse to be like you. And stay away from my momma, you hear?"

I planned to tell him that my presence in church that day was about me and my siblings—not about him and his shameful secrets. "This I vow for the rest of my life: I'm here to stay, like it or not!" I would yell.

But of course none of this happened. My momma had raised me right, so I wouldn't make a scene, not in church, and especially not on Easter Sunday.

So I imagined another possibility.

"Hey, Dad!" I'd say. "I don't want my presence here to bother you, so please forgive me for causing all this commotion in your life. If you want me to leave, I will. I'll meet my brothers and my sister somewhere else." I'd plead for forgiveness, ask him to accept me, and hope that he would invite me to be part of his family. After all, maybe this is how fathers and sons are meant to get along?

I wrestled with these competing fantasies. On the one hand,

my father deserved to hear the full extent of how his decisions had hurt me. And if I didn't unleash my feelings on him, I'd feel like a coward. On the other hand, I knew deep down I was a better man than he, and I had to act like it. Acting like a man, I knew, meant showing my father respect, even if he didn't deserve it.

In the buildup to my visit, I kept replaying the competing scenarios over and over in my mind. Then the day I had been waiting for finally arrived. Momma might not have been thrilled with my plans, but she stood by me.

It was three in the morning when she woke me. We got in the car, and we didn't talk much on the way to the bus station. As soon as I boarded the bus, I couldn't think of anything but the look on her face, the worry in her eyes that seemed to say, *My baby is leaving and entering a world that I hoped he would never know.*

When I arrived in Valdosta, my brother Johnny was there waiting for me. Once Latanya and Samantha arrived, we made our way together to the church.

The building itself was made of red brick, and seeing it made me proud to know that I was descended from people who had created such an impressive structure. We entered the church, and the first thing I noticed was a large photo of a woman I recognized as my paternal grandmother, wearing a black blouse and a red jacket. Next to her was a photo of L. B. Daniels, my grandfather, in a gray suit and glasses. I stared at the photos for a minute, thinking about the family that had been denied to me.

I retreated to the bathroom, in the front of the church, to take a moment to gather myself. I splashed water on my face. Game time.

As soon as I exited the bathroom and began walking back to the sanctuary, I saw my father.

He stood with a few other men and made introductions. I met Terry, my brother, and his half-brother. As the service began, the pastor, my uncle Roy, encouraged the congregation to hug one another. I met my other brother, Calvin, his girlfriend, Tonya, and their child, my nephew. I noticed my father standing up toward the front of the church, and he motioned for me to come up to see him. I walked over.

"Aunt Mary, this is my son Charles," he said to an older woman standing near him. We hugged, but my father motioned for me to keep moving. He had more people for me to meet.

My mind raced. Neither scenario I had played over and over again was panning out. Instead, I sat in church that Easter Sunday, unable to focus on anything the pastor preached or the choir sang. Instead, I thought about the two brothers I had just met, the aunt my father introduced me to, how my father called me his son in the presence of other people. I didn't know what to make of it all.

A few months later, on the verge of a major life change that would take me far from home, I returned to Valdosta and asked a Daniels cousin to show me my father's house. The place where he had lived for many years, with a wife and a family, hours away from me.

"Your daddy's house is the next house, on your right," my cousin Sarah told me.

I spotted it. But before I could explore more, even from a distance, Sarah pressed down on the gas. We were well on our way away from my father's house when I finally protested, "Sarah, you passed the house before I could even take a picture!"

Maybe an until-very-recently-estranged son sneaking into his father's neighborhood to take a photo of a house that was never his own makes some people feel uncomfortable. It certainly didn't seem fun for Sarah. But for me, at that moment, I needed that photo. I longed to imagine what my father's life had been like. Seeing his house was a small but, at least to me, important part of my journey.

"Boy!" Sarah shot back, "I thought you took a picture already."

She agreed to drive by the house one more time.

We looped around.

"Have your camera ready—now!" she ordered.

We drove, more slowly this time, past the house. I rolled down the window. Held my phone out the window. Snapped the photo. Sarah sped off.

Anyone else looking at that photo would think it was pretty unremarkable. The kind of image on your phone you end up deleting weeks or months after taking it, unsure why it was there to begin with. A modest, red-brick and white-vinyl-sided home. Lawn in front. Car parked in the driveway. Not unlike a million other homes spread throughout the South.

But for me, what I saw in that photo was so much more. And it hurt me to my core.

The photo shows the house where my newly discovered brothers, Calvin and Terry, grew up, with their father. My father. It shows where my father, whose presence in my life ended when I was a child, had raised a family my mother and I had known nothing about. That photo is a reminder of a life that was off-limits to me.

"Your father was always there."

Latanya's words from the previous visit bounced around in

my head. The pain was too much. I had to get out of Valdosta. Out of this entire part of the world.

Picking up the phone won't always yield the kind of feel-good moments like Sean experienced when he called his son. For me, picking up the phone led to a series of events that showed me that my father was not ready to be part of my life and that perhaps he never would be. But it was still the right decision. My father's actions showed me that the future I imagined for myself was not a possibility. But it also allowed me to see that my father's absence had little to do with me and everything to do with him. In a way, it was a healing process. While I've mourned this reality, it's given me important insight when I work with other dads.

Sometimes I can see that these dads aren't quite ready to be part of their child's life and that they could even inflict further damage if they tried too soon. I remember one man whose anger issues were still not resolved when he approached me and asked for help reconnecting with his son. I thought back to my own failed reconciliation efforts with my own father, who wasn't ready for the kind of relationship I sought. I could see how this father might further alienate his son if he didn't prepare properly for the connection. Instead, I counseled him to heal himself before taking this step, in order to avoid the kind of disappointment and hurt my own father caused me because of a premature reconciliation effort.

A desire to reconnect is a good first step, but it can't be the final step. It takes lots of work for these reconciliations to go well. Including learning the skills to recognize when your own beliefs about fatherhood might get in the way.

Lesson: As we gather in a classroom, memories linger in the air, ready to trigger a student's impulse to flee. Who among us will rise to the challenge, preventing him from reaching the door when confronted with these powerful memories? It's crucial to recognize that the subject matter that hits closest to a student's fears and pain has the potential to trigger negative beliefs and assumptions about themselves. It's important to pay close attention to this pattern and be ready to intervene to prevent destructive choices from being made as a result of that fear and pain.

8. IS MY WORTH TIED TO MY MONEY?

I 've seen firsthand in my own work and in my own life how financial stressors often magnify fatherhood's intricacies, especially within low-income communities. Studies bear this out, and it's particularly true for Black fathers, who face unique barriers stemming from economic instability and the impacts of systemic structures such as the carceral state. Two pivotal studies—one by Katie N. Russell published by *Family Relations* in 2024 and the other by Abigail Henson, also published in 2024 by *Punishment & Society*—offer invaluable insights into these challenges.

The Russell study delves into the strengths and barriers experienced by fathers, especially concerning their definitions of economic stability.[23] At the same time, Henson's report explores the repercussions of the carceral state on financial and temporal resources.[24] Together, these analyses illuminate the nature of fatherhood, financial stress, and systemic challenges, emphasizing a pressing societal issue that necessitates further exploration and action.

Russell's study reveals the perceptions of low-income Black

fathers regarding their strengths and the barriers they face. Through semi-structured focus groups, it became evident that these fathers view economic stability not merely as financial prosperity but as the fundamental ability to provide for their families. They define this stability in terms of money-management skills and their capacity to meet basic needs, such as providing food and shelter. Alarmingly, economic stability emerged as an area with more barriers than strengths, underscoring these fathers' significant challenges.

Compounding this issue is the influence of the carceral state, as detailed by Henson. The study reveals how incarceration not only disrupts the lives of fathers but also propels them into a cycle of temporal poverty. "Temporal debt" refers to the loss of time, which these fathers suffer due to legal entanglements and systemic injustices. Henson's findings suggest that the burden of time lost due to incarceration effectively bankrupts fathers, rendering them unable to meet both their financial and emotional obligations to their families.

As the studies collectively highlight, addressing the obstacles that low-income Black fathers face in achieving economic stability is fundamental for their personal development and for fostering healthier family dynamics. Tackling these issues requires a holistic understanding and innovative approaches, beyond traditional reforms aimed at easing parenting from within prison walls. Instead, we must seek systemic changes that promote economic empowerment, social support, and a deeper appreciation for the strength and resilience of fathers navigating these hurdles.

When thinking about financial and systemic challenges, one father I worked with came immediately to mind.

Cedric would not look himself in the mirror for many years after his divorce and the death of a cherished relative. Each time he tried, he could only see a pathetic alcoholic, a failure, and a staggering disappointment to his family. Someone who lacked the financial resources to care for his family. Shame, anger, and self-loathing crowded his thoughts, clouds always threatening to burst. He had grown up in a family that occupied a gentle middle ground—neither rich nor poor—where substance abuse and homelessness were mere whispers in their conversations. But he was the only one who faltered and felt those failures threaten to drown him.

One dreary day, in January 2015, reality struck Cedric with a brutal clarity. He woke up in a foreign place, beneath a twisted old tree, lying on a couch that reeked of urine. It took him a moment before he realized where he was: on his friend's discarded furniture, now a makeshift bed in her overgrown backyard.

How had he ended up here?

The question taunted him. As he lay there, the truth dawned on him: "I am homeless! My life is in the pits!"

With this realization came a stubborn resolve. Cedric had to do something, anything, to escape the pain that gripped his existence. Yet the only answer he had been able to come up with was to drown it in alcohol. Each morning, he found an excuse to buy an even bigger bottle. Days turned into weeks, but one day, even the fifth bottle of vodka he bought one afternoon failed to grant him the sweet oblivion he craved.

But Cedric just couldn't get what he longed for: complete and total blackout, just like so many times before. Instead, he slipped into a depressive haze. He was alone, homeless, scared, and cold. His hygiene stank. And he was trapped in a whirlwind of confusion, with his will to live rapidly eroding.

In those fleeting moments of despair, Cedric thought of ending his misery through suicide, dark thoughts hovering over him everywhere he went. He stood on a train platform, the metallic clamor of the approaching train reverberating through him. As he contemplated whether to leap in front of the rushing engine or lie down on the cold steel of the tracks, an unexpected thought pierced his foggy mind—*God.*

It was one of the few times in his life he found himself grappling with the concept of a higher power, yet he wasn't sure who God was to him. *How does someone reach out to whatever God may be?* he wondered.

But in that moment of desperation, Cedric decided to cast aside his uncertainty. He instinctively called out into the void, "Jesus, Allah, The Buddha, Abraham, Moses—please! Could you help me, cause I'm making my mama cry? Oh, Lord! Lord! I need help!"

Cedric didn't know who, if any, of these deities would hear him, but he felt compelled to try. And then, like a flicker of a candle in the dark, someone or something answered his prayer. It wasn't immediate, but Cedric felt the change begin to unfold.

Moments later, an older woman approached him on the platform, her kind eyes glistening with a warmth he hadn't felt in years.

"Are you okay, young man?" she asked gently.

In her presence, something deep inside Cedric began to shift. That day, he later recalled, marked a turning point. The realization blossomed within him: Life, despite its crushing lows, could still offer unexpected moments of kindness and compassion. With the eventual assistance of strangers, shelters, and the wise words of mentors he encountered on his journey, Cedric began to peel back the layers of shame and anger that had trapped him for so long. He slowly started to confront the reflection he had long avoided. Each new step—joining support groups, finding a job, and gradually reconnecting with family—dissolved the fog of despair that had engulfed him.

Years later, as Cedric stood in front of a mirror, he finally saw someone who resembled resilience and hope. No longer a failure, but a survivor. The shards of his past were indeed painful, but he learned that he could embrace the shadows as part of the journey. In his heart, Cedric discovered that faith doesn't need to be fully understood to be powerful. It was enough to reach out, acknowledge the darkness, and let the light seep in, one flicker at a time. And that flicker, however small, can eventually illuminate the path to redemption.

In a typical counseling program, Cedric would be given a set of standard assessments that weren't made for him, but which are widely used across a broad population. But what if they weren't what Cedric needed? In the same way that students are evaluated in classrooms by overly general standards, we can become victims of externally biased rankings based on society's expectations, failures, or past mistakes. Cedric and I instead focused on personal development rather than traditional assessment metrics.

Using my social work and teacher mentality, I encouraged Cedric to adopt a holistic approach to evaluating his progress. We remained fully aware of the components of the ranking system that were given to Cedric, but we acknowledged that they were created without his control or input. So instead, we worked with a concept I refer to as the *self-assessment*—an internal ranking where he measured his growth by setting benchmarks that belonged to him—and we honored his unique journey rather than comparing him to societal standards.

The focus was simple: Cedric and I created specific goals.

He practiced thinking about his life in this holistic way instead of through the lens of a rigid score that defined him. We created categories that incorporated his values and strengths while reflecting on his compassion, resilience, and even his ability to reach out for help.

Through (1) acknowledging these archaic forms of thinking and (2) dismantling them by assigning an origin to them (identifying where they came from and who contributed to their development), Cedric was able to create a framework he owned while identifying key areas of growth. He started recognizing his achievements, such as the number of days he was sober or the new connections he created in his life. He graded himself not on how he felt he had failed in the past, but on how far he had come in this moment.

Traditional grading, even in therapy and counseling, focuses on the negatives, but life is about embracing strengths and learning from those setbacks. What if we graded ourselves on how well we coexist with our mistakes and the lessons we applied from them each time? We would become more gentle with ourselves. That was part of Cedric's journey, learning to be patient and kind to himself. Or to put it another way, Cedric had to learn to be a better self-parent.

This new method of evaluation shifted Cedric's perspective entirely. He was no longer consumed by guilt and shame from past failures, which had often been prioritized at the expense of his growth. His misguided self-assessment was replaced by gratitude and recognition of the lessons he learned and the moments of success he had accomplished. In the process, he became keenly aware of the advantages and disadvantages of traditional ranking systems. Still, he learned to navigate them by focusing on how to bounce back from the cage of perceived perfection to the freedom of imperfection.

Cedric's journey serves as a testament to the idea that redemption does not lie in conforming to expectations or rigid scores, but in recognizing one's worth based on resilience and the ability to embrace change. Cedric was invited to rewrite his story—which became one of hope, transformation, and self-acceptance.

In my own life, I have tried to apply similar models of understanding to people who may have let me down at one point or another. Including my father.

I don't know what was going on in my father's mind when he joked about me visiting just to take some money off him. In retrospect, and with a whole lot of grace, I have been able to step back and consider his feelings. He had apparently felt a deep sense of shame about me and my mother, and to see me standing there with his brothers, his personal life on full display to his family, must have come as something of a shock. This isn't to excuse his behavior. But at least attempting to understand it helps me process my emotions. The moment I decided that I would no longer be the family secret, when I reached out to my uncles, met my siblings, felt like a new chapter had begun—and my father was no longer the main character. In fact, he probably felt powerless—and being powerless was something he was not used to. He'd always wielded power, often through manipulative tricks and lies. Once I took that step, inserting myself as part of his sprawling family, that power dissipated. I can only imagine how disorienting it was for him.

When I look back at my brief and sporadic encounters with my father as I was growing up, I can't help but see now how his subtle choices were influenced by experiences from his past.

The ways he chose to interact with me were infused by the hidden pain he carried with him. Regardless, the way he injected his own insecurities around money, how he used money as a cudgel in our relationship, continues to impact me in negative ways today.

Years after these encounters with my father, when he joked about money, I found it daunting to ask people for money during fundraising meetings for Fathers' UpLift. I'm not shy. Anyone who has worked with me sees my confidence and enthusiasm and would probably be shocked to learn that I feel any trepidation in asking a donor to support our work. After all, the mission is so important and the need is so great.

But whenever I had an opportunity to help bring a donor into our movement, I would freeze up. I was mentally transported back to those moments when, as a young kid, I had to muster up the courage to ask Dad for money. I worried that the donor would think all I wanted from them was money, when in reality I hoped to learn from them, to bounce ideas off them, and to spend time with them. My father's reactions to me as a child made these interactions more difficult than they should have been.

Now that I've grown up a bit and have faced financial challenges of my own, especially when raising our young children, it occurs to me that my father probably faced his own issues with money. After all, he had three families seeking resources, and while he had a good job, a single salary only goes so far. My father was with me physically when he joked about me seeking more money, but I suspect his mind was elsewhere. He was probably thinking about all the pressures in his life that having some extra money could help relieve.

At that moment, inside the hotel, my father allowed his past to control his present. If he had an angel to focus on, someone to help him through a painful and challenging moment, he wasn't keeping that in his mind's eye. He was experiencing an Internal Masculinity Conflict. An injured provider, he was reacting to his past rather than parenting his inner child, which meant he wasn't able to be a supportive father to his son. The collateral damage of financial insecurity, the stress endured by an injured provider, counted me among its victims.

In my own life, I've been fortunate to have access to tools that allow me to look at my complex emotional experiences and understand why I felt what I was feeling and how to process those feelings. Part of that experience has been an opportunity to examine how my parents and other caregivers interacted with me—and to go a step deeper and consider how their experiences were shaped by interactions and circumstances early in their lives. I've realized it's important to understand negative experiences, but also to hang on to the positive, nurturing ones as well. My parents offered me imperfect experiences, but I recognize now that they did the best they could with the emotional and financial resources they had available to them.

> **Lesson:** There are various methods of evaluating student performance in the classroom, including traditional grade ranking and our internally biased ranking systems. It's essential to understand how teachers and students use these ranking systems and analyze their advantages and disadvantages.

9. NURTURING THE INNER CHILD

Throughout my life, I've been fortunate to have caregivers who truly loved spending time with me, like my cousin Anthony and my uncle Larry. Visiting with them, I would feel safe and protected and loved. When it was time to leave, I'd feel refreshed and alive. But there were visits with other folks, like seeing my father at a gas station for a few minutes during family vacations, that didn't feel so good. Sometimes that was because the visits were so infrequent that they often felt more like work. I'd feel drained after these encounters.

Visiting our inner child can feel the same way. When I make it a point to spend time with my inner child, to seek understanding and knowledge and to take stock of his needs, I feel refreshed. If I don't, my inner child doesn't disappear, but throws a tantrum. He'll make his emotions known one way or another.

During that visit to Valdosta, my inner child wailed. The experience of seeing how close my father's family was, without ever having been invited to be part of it, was too much to bear. It made me hate everything about Georgia and made me want to flee.

Here's what I've learned spending time with my inner child over the years. I've felt his cries for years. I know what the research says about trauma. I understand the science behind it all. But there is something deeper than science happening. It is spiritual. It's what makes us human. To know the inner child is to feel and see in a new, more complete way. Understanding that I am sad and angry is one thing, but knowing the nature of the cry, its origin, is another. And my inner child has been crying for years.

That kid always wondered why his dad was not involved in his life. He wanted the answer but he couldn't bear the truth of it. Like many kids, he wasn't told the full truth because his parents were trying to protect him from a harsh reality, which was that his father didn't have the desire or the ability to be a dad to him.

That day in Valdosta, however, my mother wasn't there to protect me from the truth. All her lies about my father that she had told me growing up were useless in the face of the reality that stared me in the face. That presented a conundrum for me. My inner child held fast to the lies he had told himself, that his father was a professional athlete whose training kept him away from home. But as an adult, I was suddenly face-to-face with reality, one that made me angry. Of course my father couldn't be with me when I was a kid. He was with his other family. He couldn't be in two places at once.

These two realities collided, causing pain and discomfort in my core. My sense of self was fractured. My inner child held on to that pain and grief and wouldn't allow me to let go of it. This played out in various ways over the course of my life.

I once told Samantha that somewhere along the line, I had forgotten how to have fun. I've been a social entrepreneur for years, and in the midst of running around trying to make a difference, I put fun on the back burner. Part of my forgetting how to have fun, I realized, was linked to my neglecting my inner child.

Nurturing one's inner child must include spending time with him or her and remembering what that child enjoyed, what kinds of activities sparked joy and creativity and peace, and then considering how those activities are present as an adult. For me, I love to read and write. On most days, I'm busy running from meeting to meeting, counseling the men who come to Fathers' UpLift for guidance, and doing my best to be a good dad and husband. That doesn't leave a lot of time to spend with a good book or article, but when I can make that time, it helps to recenter me. That makes sense.

One of my earliest memories is my mom sitting down next to me and reading me books. I couldn't get enough of it; she would patiently read each page, even if she had long grown tired of reciting the same stories. She knew she was investing in my future, and she was right. At other moments, my mom's older cousin would babysit and to help pass the time, she'd sit me down and make me write my name in cursive. I'd practice and practice, spending time on each letter until the curls and loops looked perfect. It's a skill that still brings me joy today. By recollecting how important reading and writing were to me as a child, I can remember to make time for these activities as an adult so that I continue to nurture my inner child.

To put it another way, it's important for a father to parent his inner child. But parenting is a skill, and one that takes a lifetime to master. So it shouldn't come as a surprise to anyone that most fathers aren't naturals when it comes to connecting with their inner child. It takes both the awareness to know that it's important and the skill set to know how to do it well.

Parenting well means possessing the knack to confront both

joy and pain, consolation and desolation, sometimes in the same moment. When I was a child, I hid behind lies about my father, lies that my mother told me and lies that I created myself. These lies kept my pain at bay, and they even allowed me to construct some artificial joy. Telling other kids that my dad was a pro athlete traveling the world produced a rush of dopamine—even if the pain would come roaring back once that hit wore off.

Unfortunately, the inner child is left holding the pain. Especially when they come to learn the truth. And unless we do the work to help that child process and release the pain, we will eventually be held hostage to that child.

Part of nurturing my inner child has included an exercise imagining what it would look like for me to free him from the pain he still carries from childhood. I imagine what this boy would have to say when he sees the life I've created for him, what I've been able to do while he's held on to the pain. I imagine inviting him to share a meal with Samantha and our children, to sit around the table, and to be free from worry about whether his parents love him. To see that he has a mom and dad, and sisters and brothers, who love him. That he's part of a family and never has to worry about whether he is loved.

Samantha and I have moved quite a few times since we met back in college. In the midst of writing this book, we packed up our place in Boston and moved south, down to Georgia. I always tell Samantha that for me, home is wherever she and the kids are. Being with my family has helped free my inner child from some of the pain he still carries. My children love me and understand how worthy I am simply because I love them. That is their power. Because they're still young, they don't know much about what I do for work, nor about what I've been through and how that motivates my work. They do know I travel a lot, but they also know that I always come back to them. That's all. Even though my kids don't know many details of my life, they still love me.

It's a powerful thing to know that someone loves you and they will come back to you. I want my kids to know that—and I want my inner child to experience that. I think he does, because he sees how my kids' faces light up when I return after a long work trip. My father may have left me, and only returned sporadically, but I've learned I don't have to let that past affect my present. I am there when my kids need me, and my inner child has learned how it feels to be loved.

The inner child is, in all his essence, a lover. For some people, bad things happen to their inner child, and they become hard and hurt others over the course of their lives. But that's the result of running from the pain the inner child experienced, not helping him to let it go. Other people endure hardships and go on to be committed to love in order to protect other children from experiencing something similar.

I've noticed in my work counseling men to embrace their inner child that the inner child is a holder. He holds your pain even when it feels too heavy to bear. That's why when we're older, and can access the resources to process that pain, it's essential to free the inner child from the burden of carrying all that pain.

Inner children can teach us so much if we listen, if we spend time visiting with them. Life is busy and it takes effort, but when I allow myself time to visit with my inner child, and to look at my life through his eyes, I'm always amazed at what I learn about myself. I've seen this in the men I work with, too. Bringing the inner child out of the darkness and into the light is a step toward courageous self-parenting. The most challenging work as a father is trying to be the best man you can be, for yourself. That allows you to nurture your inner child, and in turn to be present for your own children. When you can't see the inner child, you can't imagine being noticed by others. When you take time to see the child how they've always longed to be seen, you give them the gift they were unable to access when they were younger. This in turn helps a man be the kind of father he knows he can be.

For fathers in particular, it's important to get to know the inner child and to envision what his life would be if he could be free from pain and trauma. I am certain that my own inner child would look at the life I've built and tell me, unequivocally: "You are worthy."

People sometimes ask me what good fatherhood means to me. I describe it as possessing the ability to bring along our inner child on the journey. When we do, we permit ourselves to feel, and we allow others to validate those feelings in our most vulnerable state. We understand and accept that vulnerability is an asset and that it symbolizes our acceptance of that inner child.

Fatherhood, in all its essence, is the gift of embracing our inner child's cries so we can be present to those who love us the most. Over the last few years, I've had the privilege and honor of working with men facing various challenges in their lives, ranging from substance abuse to being separated from their children and families. When the men come to my office, I first introduce myself, shake their hands, and look them in the eye.

Next, I begin our conversation with a clear and direct statement: "I am going to partner with you so you can become a better parent to the child in you . . ."

The responses usually contain a mixture of skepticism, confusion, and uncertainty.

"Charles, what do you mean you are going to help me parent myself . . . ?"

"I have children; I parent them."

"I'm a grown man. Do I look like I need parenting?"

While the men are almost always confused by my claim that I'm going to help them learn to parent themselves, it's become increasingly clear to me that society suffers because men are not taught about taking care of their inner child. Parenting is a foreign concept when it's used in reference to one's self. It's understandable that men don't think about parenting themselves when faced with the pressure of parenting their own kids. I get it. No one feels prepared to be a parent, and all the energy is usually focused on the kids. But when a man fails to focus on his inner child, he won't be able to be the kind of dad he wants to be.

Recognizing that your inner child, or the inner child of someone you love, is in need of love, compassion, and understanding isn't particularly difficult. It's just that most people don't know how to manage the pain that they or their loved ones experience. Often, emotional pain is a sign that the inner child is suffering. I've developed a plan for the men I work with to recognize this pain and then take steps toward healing.

First, name the pain. Once you've named the pain, take time to identify the patterns in your reactions to it. Then, write down the name or names of the pains and patterned responses in a journal or notebook. Place this information somewhere in your living space that you frequent often as a reminder. Instead of numbing the painful feeling that arises, instead of ignoring the cries of your inner child, practice speaking to yourself and your inner child in a positive and nonjudgmental manner. Then, commit to doing the opposite of what is comfortable when the painful feeling surfaces. Some painful feelings make us retreat or keep us in a box. Don't retreat. Face the pain and take steps to nurture yourself. Finally, sitting with the named pain with restraint and a nonjudgmental attitude is essential. By doing so, you will find something quite reassuring about the pain and your inner child once you have familiarized yourself with the sensations that arise.

It's necessary to approach the pain with openness and curiosity rather than fear or aversion. This practice can help people experiencing emotional pain develop a deeper understanding of the pain and its underlying causes, ultimately leading to a more peaceful coexistence with it. Embracing the discomfort with an open mind can also provide valuable insights into your mental and emotional responses to pain, allowing you to address any associated stress or anxiety more effectively.

Some people assume that parenting a child is a selfless act, and that parenting one's inner child is a selfish one. But that isn't true. It's like the airplane oxygen mask: If you don't put it on first, you won't have long to help others who need assistance putting on theirs. Parenting the inner child takes work and determination, a willingness to grapple with emotions and trauma and pain. If done well, a man will grow emotionally and learn how to cope with life's various challenges. But that's not the point. By learning to self-parent, a man will also be better able to father his children.

When I first started Fathers' UpLift, I regularly met men who had fathered children but who for various reasons just couldn't be the kinds of dads they wanted to be. I'd meet with these men and try to help them understand that before they could be good dads to their children, they needed to learn to be good parents to themselves.

This method worked particularly well with a dad named Jayden.

Jayden was just fourteen years old when he had his first child, a beautiful baby girl. Like any new parent, Jayden's life took a sudden turn. But his circumstances became particularly chaotic when, just two weeks later, he found himself in a youth detention center, sentenced to a year and a half. He remembers reassuring his parents not to worry about him, urging them to focus on his child's, their grandchild's, well-being. Jayden's parents did their best, bringing his daughter to see him each time they visited. She was shy, her small hands gripping her mother's tightly, but Jayden made sure to connect with her. He wanted his daughter to know him, even if their time together was limited.

After Jayden completed his sentence and returned home, he learned that his child's mother was pregnant again. Her declaration that she was going to keep the baby, a son, surprised Jayden. He felt overwhelmed, unsure about continuing their journey together, thinking, *I don't even know this one.*

But deep down, he knew it was beautiful; both of his children would know their father. They would grow up with him by their sides, and despite his youth, he embraced the heavy responsibility of this new chapter. Becoming a father at such a young age required divine endurance, he realized, more than he could have anticipated.

While often focused on his physical children, Jayden realized that he needed to focus on his inner child as well. He realized that all the children in his life would soak in everything he had experienced in his own life: the love, the battles, and even the resilience. But also, if he didn't get control of his ghosts, the children would absorb his trauma as well.

Jayden wanted both his son and daughter, and his child within, to feel equally cherished and seen. Their relationship with him and each other would shape their understanding of family and love.

In moments of struggle, Jayden constantly reminded himself that being a father meant being a guide and a teacher. His experiences, both painful and joyous, were lessons he wanted to pass on. He wanted his children to see that while their history may have been rife with hurdles, it was ultimately a lesson in strength and the ability to rise.

As Jayden navigated the beautiful chaos of fatherhood, he strived to create a nurturing atmosphere where both of his physical children, and his inner child, could flourish. By embracing that ethos, he was able to foster a love that stretched beyond him, one that could be felt by everyone in his family. It was a labor of love, breaking cycles and building new foundations, knowing that his children would be learning and growing alongside him.

Jayden now finds solace in the fact that he has the power to shape the narratives of his children and his inner child, to write a future where love prevails over chaos and where the lessons of empathy, understanding, and connection transcend generations.

As a partner in Jayden's journey, I understood the importance of being attentive to the dynamics within Jayden's wider family and helped him draw parallels to his experiences in the "classroom," or the counseling office. I had to emphasize again and again that Jayden must always strive to remember that there is more than one student in that room—even when it was just him and me talking.

There was Jayden himself, as well as his inner child, who felt angry, nervous, and neglected, especially when recalling moments when his parents fought nonstop during his own childhood. If Jayden didn't confront this pain that he still carried, it was likely he would pass it on to his children.

I encouraged Jayden to embrace his children (the ones within and outside of him) as unique individuals, highlighting that each child carries their own voice, shaping his family's interactions. I guided him to take the time to understand the importance of quality moments with both his physical children, and his inner child, even if one seemed more prominent in his mind.

"Your child within may seem like the main student now," I told him. "But your babies in the flesh will be better off once you embrace the memories of that child, as they are also watching and learning from you. You need to connect with both; they will influence each other and you as their father."

Through role-playing and other exercises, I showed Jayden how to engage meaningfully with each child during their visits, ensuring they felt valued and understood. I taught him to ask open-ended questions, providing opportunities for expression. This strategy fostered a connection and allowed Jayden to appreciate the different perspectives and emotions they brought into their family dynamic.

Jayden discovered that he wasn't just shaping his and his children's lives, but enriching his understanding of fatherhood by paying attention to his inner child. The lesson in our work here was that the true essence of connection lies in recognizing the nuances of every child's perspective, even the one you can't see physically but feel. In doing so, Jayden found strength in his role as a father. Every interaction matters, and every "student" in the room, even the one in the back of the classroom out of sight, deserves to be seen and embraced.

Through my work in the mental health space, I saw firsthand that there were few materials available to support individuals with tending to the child within. Or what I call "Parenting the Child Within."

As I explained to Jayden, and the hundreds of other men like him I've worked with over the years, the physical child that meets the eye is not the only child present. The child within is always present, and age doesn't negate their experiences.

We typically associate a certain age with signaling the transition from childhood to adulthood. Maybe it's eighteen, when most people graduate high school, or twenty-one, when one can order a drink legally. But no number can fully erase the experiences a person has as a child.

Most people can probably remember the first time they had their heart broken. For lots of us, this happens during the teenage years. We might find a partner and think we'll be together forever. But summers end, graduations arrive, and that love is cut short. The heartache can feel unbearable in the moment, but most of us move on. But maybe later in life, another relationship fails. We might feel overcome with anger and grief and fear. The child within us suddenly reasserts him or herself and we're transported back to that first moment of heartache. That inner child has captured our past and stored it within the very fabric of our being. If we don't learn how to interact with and parent that child, they'll rule our lives and inform the decisions we make.

It was with this in mind that I realized that if I was going to serve anyone, whether professionally or even in my personal life, I had to look beyond their present circumstances and get to know their inner child. One way or another, that inner child is dictating the choices they make, how they respond to conflict, and how they live day-to-day. That child has a name, a preference, and a voice.

Part of my life's work has been to encourage both individuals and the field of parenting preparedness to take the inner child more seriously. I want us to shift the conversation from solely dealing with the challenges that accompany the parenting of other people, usually kids, to first learning how to parent the child within. Being a parent to another child, or a partner to another person, without first tending to the child within is a fool's errand. It's just not going to work.

Negligence is a form of unhealthy parenting, and it applies to our inner child as well as our actual children. Whenever I work with the men who come to me for counseling, I urge them to see the "child in the room" by pausing, looking, and greeting that child with love and hospitality, rather than disdain and dismissiveness.

Some of us suppress the child's cries when memories of trauma surface. That's only natural. Dealing with past trauma is scary and takes work. Sadly, many of us run from the inner child's existence because his or her presence is unbearable. There are various ways of coping, consciously and subconsciously, which are essential tools in learning to navigate the complexities of life.

Instead of neglecting the inner child, or pretending they don't exist, emotionally healthy adults should be able to name the child, identify his or her experiences, and treat the child with love and compassion.

Countless numbers of people have successfully parented individuals from childhood to adulthood. In some ways, it isn't remarkable. These individuals have gone on and done great things with their lives. But when we think of everything that life can throw one's way, it's nothing short of miraculous that people are able to grow into healthy, functioning adults, and then care for their children, too. Imagine the possibilities if more of us were to take a parenting approach to dealing with the child within. What kind of world would we live in if we began to honor parenting of the inner child in a similar way that we honor external parenting?

As a society, we punish parents who do not fit the typical description of a "good and safe parent." What if we were also punished for the way we treat ourselves? Many of us would pay a steep penalty.

Dads often ask me how they can identify their inner child's needs. I usually tell them that it starts by reflecting on the following questions:

1. What was the location of the most harmful event in your life? This is the memory of an emotionally devastating event. We often have experienced multiple situations that have been painful, but there is one or two, or even more, that feels like a clanging gong in your ear every time you think of it. Find that first location.
2. Who were the actors involved? This could be you, somebody else from your life, or both.
3. What made this event injurious?
4. Finally, when does this event trigger a reaction in the present? For instance, a memory of feeling abandoned by a loved one leads to prematurely cutting off people trying to get to know you to avoid the same feeling from resurfacing or a similar outcome from occurring.

Once these questions are answered, I ask the man to describe a characteristic of his inner child. The first step to parenting the child within is to understand how he operates. I encourage the man to do this for every event that he carries internally.

Healing occurs by identifying the ways that he wishes traumatic events had actually played out. For instance, in Jayden's case, he said he wished his home life had been more stable while he was growing up. The fear he experienced when his parents fought scarred Jayden's inner child, and he carried those wounds with him when he became a parent himself. I encouraged Jayden to imagine a different reality for his inner child, so that he could reshape his present circumstances.

The idea of nurturing an inner child might feel foreign or even silly, especially for men who have been taught by society to ignore their emotional lives. But I always tell the men I work with that I know firsthand the benefits of seeking to understand the child within, and that it's a worthwhile practice. Imagine the inner child as a friend, I suggest, someone who is no longer a stranger, who no longer sits alone at the lunch table, far away from what we deem worthy of our time and attention in our busy lives. Through this, we can learn to treat ourselves more gently and with greater kindness.

Not only have I noticed the importance of tending to the cries of the child within with compassion, honesty, and forgiveness, but I have also had to work with my own inner child while assisting hundreds of men in my clinic. The best thing that anyone has ever done for me, and my inner child, was to stand up for me. By focusing on examples of real-life people standing up for me when I was a child, I can help my inner child continue to build confidence and put him on the path to healing.

I remember it like it was yesterday. I was ten years old, in my hometown church in College Park, Georgia. I was on the verge of being baptized in the church I attended every Sunday morning with my mother. That morning, I woke up and got dressed before riding to church with my mother, our regular

Sunday morning routine. But this particular morning was special.

When we arrived at the church, my mother escorted me to the back of the church, where the other children were getting dressed in the garments that would serve as their baptismal robes. I was the last person to arrive.

Once dressed, I met the rest of the children in the lobby with the deacon who would facilitate the ceremony. I peeked from the lobby into the sanctuary to see all the people waiting for the service to begin. Then, with the service about to start, I ran back to my place in the line and waited for the pastor to signal to us that it was time to go to the front of the church. Once it came, we proceeded down the aisle in a straight line, passing all the family members of the boys and girls who were being baptized that day. By the time I regained my focus, we were standing at the front of the church.

"Charles," the pastor called out, before wrapping his arms around me.

Before asking me to turn to face the congregation, the pastor asked me if I was all right. I don't recall if he sensed my trepidation or if he could feel that sinking feeling overtaking me, as I gleaned around the church and saw everyone else's families there to support them. For me, it was just my mom.

With both of us now facing the congregation, the pastor asked, "Will the family of this boy please stand?"

I looked out into the congregation and saw my mother, standing alone in what felt like a sea of people sitting down.

The pastor looked at me, then again out into the congregation.

With more conviction, he asked the congregants again, "Will the family of this young man stand!" This time, it was less of a question and more of a command.

Everyone inside that church stood up. What could have been a scarring experience for that young child, me, instead transformed into a moment of healing and hope.

When those in the congregation stood up that morning, it was more than a simple physical reaction to the pastor's request. It was a commitment, conveying to me and the world that they would love that child standing in front of them. They saw me and I felt seen. After enduring years of wondering why my own father didn't wish to see me, I took solace in the fact that this community of women and men saw me and loved me. That experience in the church remains an angel moment for me, nurturing my inner child in times of self-doubt. Making time to recall this experience is a positive act of self-parenting. But it takes a lot of self-reflection to distill our past experiences down to angels and ghosts, tools that we can use to parent the inner child.

It's imperative that we know who's talking when we are in an emotional bind. Are we upset about something in our lives, or is the inner child reliving a past trauma? It's important to know the difference. The inability to do so could lead to childish decisions and repeated moments of lashing out.

Next, we must be able to identify the reasons why the inner child cries. Every person has things he or she likes and dislikes. Children may demonstrate this by smiling at one moment and shrieking in another. Adults might have more sophisticated methods of expressing their emotions. But it's important to understand that there are certain experiences that bring comfort and others that cause pain. What makes that inner child vulnerable?

Painful moments we endured as children can serve as indicators for how we might act as adults. These moments leave us with beauty marks that remind us of what we experienced back then, every time we feel them now. Cries can be annoying and easily cause discomfort, especially when they continue for an extended period. But if left unattended, those cries don't go anywhere.

Essential to being able to parent the child within is the ability to recognize when the inner child needs your attention, your voice. There may be emotional or physical places you cannot go because you are reminded of what you experienced every time you visit those places. There may be a group of people that you cannot work with given your past experiences. Those are the cries. They represent your inner child's hurt. It is important that you hold on to that and remember what those moments represent, so that you can remain aware of the sound of the cry.

There's a flip side to this, too. Focusing on what brings the inner child joy can help us make better decisions in our lives today. I remember how happy I was as a child when competing on the football field, taking pride in my athletic ability and loving it when our team prevailed over the competition. Or a meal that brought comfort, like when my mom would make macaroni and cheese. As a child, I couldn't get enough of it. Whenever we'd visit my grandmother and relatives in West Palm Beach, I found joy.

Still to this day, Florida remains a special place where I travel with my wife and children to see family and visit the places I spent time at as a child. When I'm back in those special places, my inner child is at peace, and I'm able to be present in a healthy, nourishing way with Samantha and our children.

What are the joys for your inner child? These memories are a part of you. Honor them. To ignore the identity of the child is to ignore an important aspect of your being. This will be essential in helping to meet the needs of the inner child, and to help that child heal. It's especially important to learn to recognize your inner child's voice.

Often, when children speak, they have a voice that only their parents will be able to identify. They also have messages that they are attempting to convey when they are speaking to us. Sometimes a toddler only needs to make a seemingly unintelligible noise to communicate with a parent, and the parent will know immediately what their child is trying to convey. It can be similar with the inner child.

For your inner child, their voice often comes as a whisper. But then we follow that whisper with an action. The whisper is typically the message that makes gentle inferences, and assumptions, without any tangible evidence. The only evidence that we hear in that whisper is what's connected to our past experiences.

For example, let's say you experienced issues of abandonment when you were a child and that recently, you've been developing a relationship with a new friend. The level of commitment that you give to that new relationship could potentially be hindered by that whisper you hear that is linked to what you experienced as a child. Inferences display themselves through the child's whispers, such as subtle messages like "be careful, people will hurt you, just like you were hurt when you were a child."

Those messages have power, and typically, they can prevent us from even being able to see the possibilities of what new relationships can bring. The whisper jumps to a conclusion with illegitimate evidence for us to use.

The only evidence that the inner child considers legitimate when they are in pain is their past experiences. Specifically, the experiences that have left them deeply hurt. How we reply to those whispers makes all the difference. We respond to the voice with an action, and moments when the inner child thinks that they are in control are the moments when we act on their illegitimate messages. These can be disastrous moments for us, because we feel like we are doing what we want, but in reality, we are making decisions based on an inaccurate set of circumstances.

Remember, the inner child operates solely from the vantage point of something that happened to them in the past. A common sign that we are being parented by the child is when we engage in avoidant behavior. The child can be very fearful and convince us not to try new things based on a few select, negative experiences. The scarred inner child keeps us in the box, stagnant, stuck in one place. When we act based on that whisper, we remain stuck where the hurt took place.

Let's say an individual, a friend or family member perhaps, suddenly left us when we were a child. For me, my dad's occasional presence when I was young, followed by long stretches of absence, shaped my childhood. You might have your own situation, but whatever that moment of hurt is for you, it remains part of your foundation, even well into adulthood.

The directive that comes with the child's whisper is a subtle defense mechanism that protects the inner child from once again feeling vulnerable. The directive can convince us that a situation is dangerous, even if it's simply unfamiliar. If we're not careful, the inner child will control us, as opposed to us, the adults, acting as parents. Learning to distinguish the inner child's cry from our own thoughts about a given situation is how we regain control. But being the parent is hard. I've found it helpful to remember that there is no such thing as the perfect parent. But there *is* such a thing as a parent who fully embraces every aspect of their child. To be the parent of the child, we must have an awareness of the various characteristics of the child.

To parent the inner child, we must accept the moments the child will make us vulnerable. Understanding that we don't need to give in to every demand from the inner child will position us to parent effectively.

These realities can be difficult to accept, especially in the context of modern life that seemingly gives us control over nearly every challenge we might encounter. There are surgeries to give us six-pack abs, medications to lessen the effects of seasonal colds, and substances that numb us to the pains of everyday life. But when it comes to the inner child, none of these interventions will work. The child within cannot be removed with a surgical procedure or silenced with a pill. The child is the only person that remains a part of our being, and there is nothing that can rid us of it.

My approach has always been this: Learn to live with your inner child, rather than try to ignore them. Embracing the existence of our experiences and what the child represents is key to any parenting experience.

Take the story of Kenneth, another dad I worked with to help him name his pain and nurture his inner child.

Kenneth wore many hats: a devoted dad, a caring friend, and an employee who worked tirelessly to make ends meet. However, beneath the surface, he struggled with his relationship with alcohol. A friend, noticing his troubles, referred him to me. At first, Kenneth was reluctant to admit he had a problem.

"I do what I must do when I have to. Drinking is not an issue," he insisted.

However, the looming threat of permanently losing custody of his son began to weigh heavily on his heart. That's why he agreed to open up to me.

In our initial meetings, Kenneth shared his daily routine. Each morning began with a drink to kick-start his day, then another to help him push through, and one more at night to unwind. This was the format of his life, a necessary evil in his mind but nonetheless, he felt, necessary. But when I asked him to articulate why, he struggled.

"My son, Kenneth Jr., will not be coming home," he said.

Through gentle questioning, I helped Kenneth see his drinking in a different light. I asked him to imagine that the person who needed all those drinks to get through the day was not Kenneth, but his inner child. I asked Kenneth to name that child. After some reflection, he chose a name that struck a chord—"Ellis." This personification of his addiction, with deeper roots to a looming pain, allowed him to separate himself from his destructive habits, giving the addiction a face.

This character, Ellis, had been lurking in the shadows of Kenneth's life.

"Ellis's cries have been present all along," Kenneth acknowledged. "He led to my loss of custody, my drinking. Ellis is like an old friend who never has my best interest at heart."

Kenneth recognized how Ellis intertwined with feelings of shame, failure, and anger, particularly in the context of fatherhood.

"Every time I interact with Ellis and with his pain, I feel pushed into a negative space, and it prevents me from being the dad I want to be," Kenneth said.

As our sessions progressed, Kenneth began to confront Ellis rather than hide from him. He learned to articulate how the effects of Ellis spilled onto every aspect of his life, especially his relationship with his son. Together, Kenneth and I worked through the emotions that bubbled to the surface: disappointment in the child welfare system, the frustration of unexpected delays in getting his son back, and regretting past decisions.

Kenneth's journey took work. There were days filled with setbacks and old habits beckoning him to return. But with relentless support, he learned the power of vulnerability, the freedom that came with acknowledging his struggles and fears rather than masking them with alcohol. He began to find healthier coping mechanisms, such as talking through his emotions, which allowed him to feel emotions without being overwhelmed by them.

Ellis slowly lost some of his power over Kenneth's life. Bit by bit, Kenneth revealed layers of himself that had long been buried under a guise of bravado and denial. He started to realize that reclaiming his identity as a father meant addressing the demons that clouded his mind and heart.

In time, the clouds of despair began to lift. He found camaraderie with others in our network who faced similar battles. He shared stories of his dreams and envisioned a future where they could be together, free from the shadow of Ellis and his pain. With perseverance, determination, and a newfound understanding, Kenneth rewrote his story. He wanted to illustrate to his son that while the road to recovery was long, it was filled with hope and possibility. Every step forward became a testament to his commitment to healing—not just for himself, but for his son. He felt a strength he hadn't known as his journey progressed. He was not defined by Ellis's pain but rather by his efforts to reclaim his life and be the father he always aspired to be. He transformed his narrative from loss to redemption, proving that it's never too late to seek help and strive for a brighter future.

The journey of self-discovery and transformation deepened as Kenneth continued to separate himself from "Ellis" and his pain. He began to recognize his profound power over this symbolic figure, realizing that it was not a permanent part of his identity but a challenge to confront head-on. A pivotal discussion unfolded during one session, when Kenneth recalled a moment when Ellis seemed to take control over his life.

"I remember when the case worker called me out of the blue that day, when I was out with my father at the bar," Kenneth reflected. "In the past, I would not have answered the phone. But I knew she was calling me about my son. So I answered. She asked me to meet her somewhere, and I did."

Kenneth admitted he was under the influence, but he showed up anyway because his son meant that much to him. Inquiring further, I asked, "How did you manage not to let Ellis and his pain prevent you from showing up at that moment?"

His voice trembled slightly as he shared, "I had been hiding for a long time. Sometimes, Ellis knocked me down, and I stayed down. But my boy was in a foster home. Every second I stayed down was another second added to my son's time there. I had to get up even when I was down."

Tears rolled down his face, but with each drop he felt a weight lift.

"Junior needs me to stand up and stare down Ellis," Kenneth continued, his voice now more resolute.

Kenneth acknowledged that "Ellis" still spoke to him daily, whispering temptations and reminding him of his past failures. Yet, he also recognized what he was truly fighting for: his son's future, their reunification, and the possibility of healing their fractured relationship.

After several sessions, Kenneth noticed that his urge to use alcohol dissipated. With improved coping skills, he was better equipped to handle stress, anxiety, and the daily challenges of life. His determination to fight for his son grew more assertive as their bond remained in his heart, driving every decision he made. Then came the day that would change everything: He received the news that he had regained custody of his son. Ellis would never leave, but Kenneth had learned how to hear his voice and how to take actions that weren't dominated by Ellis's pain.

The day Kenneth reunited with Junior, he experienced a flood of emotions. Relief, joy, apprehension, and an overwhelming sense of responsibility. Standing before his son, Kenneth knew the battle was worth every tear he had shed and every moment he had forced himself to face Ellis.

Often, though, learning to heal from the pain still carried by the inner child is an impossible task to do our own. It requires a team of folks, friends, family, and even counselors and coaches, to be able to find wholeness.

Lesson: Perspective is essential. Create a space that allows the inner child to coexist with the student. This way, when they make mistakes, we can understand their struggles and the situation as a whole. Don't label the student as anything other than a human being. When the child cries or acts out, it's crucial to remind them that crying is a natural human reaction and doesn't define who they are. We want to foster an environment where each student feels understood and appreciated for who they are.

10. DON'T ALLOW YOUR PAST TO DICTATE YOUR FUTURE

An integral part of being present is listening deeply to the pain, concerns, and hopes of the person in front of you. I've learned how this kind of deep listening can transform lives, in part because of people who took the time to listen to me. As I said earlier, sometimes a father simply cannot be in the lives of his children. But that doesn't mean that others can't step up to fill the father role. Those individuals can make all the difference. I know because I've benefited from many such relationships, including one that arrived during a particularly challenging and formative time in my life. I still use lessons from that father figure today, especially when it comes to how I approach coaching and counseling, particularly in teaching men how to listen.

Arriving as an undergrad at Cookman, the scope of what I was about to take on weighed on me. I had always enjoyed school, and my love of learning could be traced back to the books my mom read to me as a young child. I knew that many people had sacrificed for me to be here, and I took that seriously. So seriously, in fact, that even in the hot and humid Daytona, Florida, weather, I decked myself out in a three-piece suit. My goal was to show that I was a young man on the move, that someday soon, I would be somebody. I didn't have much money, as evidenced by the holes worn through the bottoms of my dress shoes, but nobody had to know that. Dressed up and walking with purpose, I set out to make my mark at Cookman.

This wasn't always easy. I didn't have many role models at home to help me navigate the unspoken rules of college life. But I had plenty of mentors, accomplished and caring women and men on campus who took time to show me the ropes. They saw potential in me and wanted to help me succeed. In many ways, the men were father figures for me when my own father seemingly wanted nothing to do with me.

One of those men was Dr. Anthony Owens.

Dr. Owens worked in student services and became something of a coach for me as I navigated college life. His patience and encouragement were indispensable as I figured out who I wanted to be and how I could shape that version of myself. But most of all, I remember a bit of advice he gave me on more than one occasion, moments when I felt like I couldn't get my life on track no matter how hard I tried.

When I was in college, in the early 2000s, I was navigating several personal issues all at once. My mom's health was in decline and I saw how she, as a middle-aged Black woman, was shunted aside by the healthcare system, unable to access the treatments and care that she needed. My own mental health challenges, stemming in part from the anger I felt toward my father, simmered and eventually boiled over, requiring me to spend time addressing my emotions in a more systemic manner. When I told Dr. Owens everything that was going on, he encouraged me to keep going. But how could I have a future, I wondered, when everything in my life seemed so shaky and unstable?

"Don't allow your past," Dr. Owens told me, "to dictate your future."

It's a fairly simple maxim, but those few words really did change my attitude and ultimately the trajectory of my life.

I couldn't run from the challenges or from my past, and Dr. Owens helped me realize that I was not a prisoner to my circumstances, that I could choose to acknowledge my pain without letting it control me or set my future. When things didn't go the way I hoped, I could choose to sulk and use my past as a plausible excuse—or I could choose to move forward.

During college, there were several times when I thought, *This just isn't for me.*

Football had played a central role in my life up to this point. The competitiveness of trying to win, the rush of endorphins following a successful play, the outlet for aggression—all that had been so important to me growing up. That drive helped get me through high school. Plus, it connected me to my father, who had been a successful football player himself. When I enrolled at Cookman, I planned to make my mark as a successful college athlete. Before that could happen, I had to pass a trigonometry class in order to be eligible to play. That summer, at nearby Daytona College, I did my best to understand triangles and ratios and complex formulas, but it felt so useless. No matter how hard I tried, I just couldn't muster up the energy to care. As a result, I didn't do very well. Trig was not for me.

I remember telling the professor how I needed to pass this course so that I could play football. I told him how important it was for me to pass so I could join the team. Scholarship money would open up, I said, and I'd get the chance to make friends and travel more. My world would expand, and everything was riding on this course.

"I really need this credit," I told the professor, a middle-aged, thin white man whose life seemed so different from my own. "Because I really want to play football."

"Well, maybe you can coach Little League," he said to me, with a hint of sarcasm that really rubbed me the wrong way.

I failed the course. Just like that, my dreams of gridiron glory went down the tubes. The professor's lack of encouragement left me angry.

At twenty or so, forging an identity is no easy task. Free from the confines of home for the first time, young adults try to figure out who they are and who they want to be. Though it might have been shortsighted in retrospect, my identity then had been wrapped up in being a college football player. And now, because of a single math class, the future I envisioned for myself was out of reach.

"Dr. Owens, I'm gonna quit everything," I remember telling him.

Dr. Owens didn't let me sulk.

"Charles," I remember him saying, "you have a deeper purpose than football. You came here to get a degree, not to play football."

Even if I felt like giving up, this man saw something in me that I couldn't quite envision myself. And because of his kindness and encouragement, I didn't give up. This scenario played out many more times during the next few years.

Dr. Owens recognized that I needed some wins, especially during the first couple of years at Cookman, when nothing seemed to be going right. He encouraged me to explore a new initiative on campus, the Black Males in Higher Education Think Tank. The goal of the organization was to prepare young Black men on campus for the professional world, giving us opportunities to meet with activists and leaders from the wider community in order to learn important skills and shape our character before we left campus. Following Dr. Owens's advice, I joined the group and valued the relationships I built. Most of them anyway. One faculty member just didn't like me. As an adult, I realize now that was his problem, not mine. But as a college student, his attitude really made me question myself. My ideas weren't appreciated, my contributions minimized. I just couldn't seem to get a fair shake.

I didn't know how to handle this conflict, and I told Dr. Owens how unfair it all felt. I leaned on him like a crutch, and he held me upright. He listened to my frustrations and helped me understand my own value, even when others didn't quite see it. He gave me the space to acknowledge what was going on, without trying to fix everything, and encouraged me to keep going.

And he also gave me a piece of practical advice.

"Charles, if you don't like what's going on," I can hear him telling me, "go do something about it."

He suggested I go talk to the president of the college at the time, Dr. Trudie Kibbe Reed.

"Am I good enough to talk to the president of a college?" I wondered aloud. "Am I really good enough to have a difficult conversation with such an accomplished adult?"

Despite my self-doubt, Dr. Owens encouraged me to make an appointment. I did so, and when I entered Dr. Reed's office, I told her what was going on in the Think Tank. She listened patiently and thanked me for expressing my concerns.

That meeting didn't change the dynamic in the Think Tank. But with the benefit of hindsight, I don't think that was the reason why Dr. Owens encouraged me to meet with President Reed. While I still had issues with a particular faculty member who seemed bent on not liking me, I nonetheless learned that

I was indeed good enough to meet with someone as important as Dr. Reed. In fact, the two of us went on to develop a friendship that lasted the rest of my time in college. It was simple advice, to stand up for myself when I felt I was being treated unfairly, but advice I would not have received had Dr. Owens not taken time to listen to me, to care about me, to father me.

When I talked to Dr. Owens years later, as I was writing this book, I had the rare opportunity to tell a mentor how much his encouragement had meant to me as a young man. How the meals in his home that he invited me to provided a sense of stability during a particularly tumultuous time in my life. That conversation was a gift. I know that I am far from the only graduate of Cookman who feels like he had a uniquely special relationship with Dr. Owens—after all, he's worked in student affairs at Cookman for more than twenty years. But I was curious how he connected with me and other students in such profound ways.

Part of it might be his own background.

Dr. Owens's fatherhood journey started in Jacksonville, Mississippi, where he was one of fourteen children raised by his father and grandfather. In a home filled with love, but limited resources, he observed these two remarkable men opening their hearts and home to children in their neighborhood, treating them as their own. This early model of selfless love and support planted the seeds of his lifelong commitment to encouraging young people.

As he told me years later, "It all stemmed from seeing my dad, that untrained professional social worker, really being a social worker. [He] had so many kids, and [I saw] how he maneuvered and had all of us busy at one time, and all of us turned out well."

It's not easy to remember the specifics of my interactions

with Dr. Owens during my college years. Too much time has passed. But I can still feel how his words encouraged me, built me up, helped me to see the value in myself. During casual dinners at Piccadilly Cafeteria, over in Daytona Beach, Dr. Owens told me over and over that the challenges I faced weren't my fault. There was constant affirmation about my abilities and his regular refrain that my dad's absence was not my fault. He redirected me away from dwelling on my past, and I'm grateful for the grace that allowed me to receive his advice with appreciation. My own father may not have been there to give me the encouragement I needed, but Dr. Owens was.

Dr. Owens volunteers today with Fathers' UpLift, and his wisdom and gentle encouragement are aiding another generation of young men seeking to embrace their own potential. Many of the men Dr. Owens coaches through Fathers' UpLift come from circumstances that might reasonably hold them back or prevent them from living the kind of lives they want for themselves and their families. But they are fortunate to have at their disposal the words Dr. Owens told me decades ago, that I have now let seep deep into my own psyche.

I actually have the power not to let my past determine my future.

Pain is a heavy and emotional experience we all carry. Its origin may differ from person to person, but we all feel the effects no matter how pain enters our lives. Tracking how pain influences our emotions is a helpful way to process trauma. When I was a young man and felt overwhelmed by pain, Dr. Owens's resounding message to me was an important reminder that people can rise beyond the feelings associated with our most painful circumstances.

Dr. Owens was convincing enough, and persistent enough,

that I eventually believed him. Whenever I get too wrapped up in my own head, I remind myself that my past circumstances do not determine the outcome of my future. Truthfully, I never knew that it was possible for a person to gain control of their future after a traumatic and painful situation. I thought that each of us was dealt a hand of cards and that we had no choice about the game. Now, I have come to know that although we can't choose our circumstances, we can choose to lead a life in control. I've learned to treat the emotional damage that follows a painful moment as a neighbor that I learn to like, or at least tolerate, despite the discomfort that it brings. Reminding ourselves that we are in control has to be constant. These reminders come in the form of our words and translate into beliefs that can carry us through life—if we use them regularly. We owe ourselves a reminder that we are in control of the present anytime we are bound by the past.

Being present means not attempting to numb the pain as if we are powerless in our current context.

Sometimes when I'm in a tough spot, I treat Dr. Owens as one of my angels. I focus on him telling me, "Feel what you feel, but don't be defined by it," or, "Your purpose is much greater than this moment of pain," or, "In fact, the pain you are experiencing now is an important part of your journey; what if there was something special in that terrible moment?"

This example of being present was, at that point, foreign to me. For the first couple of decades of my life, I felt like my circumstances controlled me, that I was always reacting to other people's decisions. But Dr. Owens showed me what it meant to exercise transformational presence, how the art of being present shapes those around us.

Looking back on my many conversations with Dr. Owens, I see now that his message can be summed up using these words: *Being present includes embracing pain with a gentle and stern conviction.* The role we play as presence-holders is like water: It flows wherever the wind blows and can move within various spaces, no matter how big or small.

It might sound cliche, but Dr. Owens's presence in my life changed everything. I've carried with me his lesson that the power of being present can help us see beyond our pasts. Each time I was triggered by my past trauma, which contributed to repetitive questioning of my worth, Dr. Owens remained attentive to the moment he was sharing with me. His message gracefully reminded me of the power I possess to overcome each fleeting moment of self-doubt and hopelessness. His gestures reminded me that I am the victor, not the victim. How could this have occurred if his presence was laden with ridicule and judgment? Would I eventually grow to conclude that I was capable of being anything other than a worthless "love child"? The room for alternative consideration was small, but his approach to being present was much more extensive and agile. His presence created room for healing in a small and confined space of my heart. Being present is not loud and egocentric. It's actually the opposite: quiet, consistent, and, when done right, compressible.

Unfortunately, not every man will have a Dr. Owens in his life to help keep him on the right path and impart valuable lessons that he will carry over into fatherhood. But there are a few takeaways that can help men be better dads. I've used these ideas in my own coaching.

One of the main lessons is taking time to listen deeply.

Listening deeply, either to a dad in need of help or to a child longing for connection with his or her father, takes effort, especially when daily life seems to get in the way. But the payoff can be huge. Listening deeply fosters emotional connection, encourages open communication, and enhances problem-solving skills.

I always tell dads that listening deeply is a skill that can be learned. Here's how.

First, it's important to offer your full attention. That means putting aside distractions, making eye contact, and showing physically that you're only focused on the conversation happening at this moment.

Next, respond to concerns with empathy. Acknowledge expressed feelings and make an effort to show that you are at least seeking to understand their point of view.

Finally, asking open-ended questions is an invitation to share more, to be vulnerable. Asking, "How did that make you feel?" may prompt important moments of self-reflection.

It won't be obvious in the moment the impact that deep listening makes, and it's unlikely that a single conversation will ever be truly life-altering. But those conversations add up, and the cumulative impact can be transformative.

> **Lesson:** What you thought you knew is not always accurate. That's why deep listening is so essential. Whenever students create stories about themselves with limited information, inaccuracies are inevitable. It's crucial to identify these gaps to prevent them from distorting the narrative.

11. FORGIVING OUR PASTS

Forgiveness is often an essential but tricky part of the healing journey for many of the men who turn to us for help at Fathers' UpLift. Necessary, because without forgiveness, individuals often remain stuck in the past, replaying traumatic events over and over in their minds. Tricky, because letting go of pain, whether caused by one's own actions or somebody else's, sometimes feels like surrendering. Either way, working on forgiveness is key. The stories of two dads I've worked with serve as helpful models of how forgiving events and people from our pasts can radically transform our futures.

As a young father, Zephaniah was filled with joy and pride the day his daughter called out for him the first time. As he held her, with her two little pigtails bouncing and her sweet, innocent lisp ringing in his ears—"Daddy, Daddy, I love you!"—a transformation unfolded within him. He was young and uncertain, yet nothing felt as profound as this moment. His life had taken on new meaning, and he vowed to be the protector she needed.

But the tides of life can be cruel.

A devastating loss shattered Zephaniah's world when he received the call that no parent wants to hear. His baby girl had been in a car accident. Rushing to the hospital, desperation consumed him. Then, once he arrived, he was met with an unbearable reality. Zephaniah's daughter had passed away before he could hold her again.

The days that followed were a blur of heartache. Numbed by all that had happened, Zephaniah made decisions no father should ever make. He chose an outfit for his daughter's funeral, a beautiful white and pink dress, and adorned her with a delicate crown. The sight of the custom-made pink casket, inscribed with the word "princess," haunted his dreams in the months that followed his daughter's funeral. Isolation set in, and the walls of despair slowly closed around him. With his heart filled with agony and no way to cope, he turned to substances to numb his pain, drowning in the depths of addiction.

Friends and family turned away, and soon, Zephaniah found himself homeless, with a mere twenty dollars to his name. He felt like a ghost, wandering through life with few remnants of hope. The only escape he saw for himself was either jail or death.

Yet, beneath the layers of despair, memories of a brighter past tugged at him. Thoughts of his daughter played like a haunting melody, a bittersweet reminder of the joy that once was. In the depths of his struggle, he realized that while he was grappling with the painful loss of his daughter, he had another family waiting for him—a loving wife who had steadfastly refused to give up on him, and even other children who needed him. But Zephaniah was angry, not at a particular person, but at the events that surrounded his daughter's death. He couldn't see how he would ever be able to forgive.

Zephaniah remembered other people labeling him as broken, but even in the grip of his grief, he wouldn't allow himself to accept such definitions for himself. He embraced the lesson that everyone experiences both struggles and triumphs. Through therapy, and the tireless support of his wife, he began allowing himself to grieve, reminding himself that his tears were a natural human reaction. With every drop that fell, he felt a little lighter, slowly breaking free from the chains of addiction that had bound him.

Struggles pushed him forward. He learned to express his love openly with each of his children, finding joy in their laughter and warmth in their hugs. Their smiles became his refuge, his reminder that he was still important, still worthy of love. Whenever he would announce, "I love you!" to his children, their bright, beaming faces lit up, a reflection of the bond that emerged stronger than ever.

I'm not sure if Zephaniah ever truly forgave the circumstances that led to his daughter's death, but he at least learned that his life did not need to be defined by that experience. He became a testament to resilience, embodying the truth that pain and joy can coexist. Though he still carried the scars of loss, Zephaniah learned to rise again. Each time he looked into his children's eyes, he was reminded of the little girl who had changed his life forever, inspiring him to cherish every precious moment as a dad.

In partnering with Zephaniah, I applied a few seemingly simple lessons that helped him rise.

UNDERSTANDING EMOTIONS

I encouraged Zephaniah to embrace all emotions, including crying, as natural and valid. I reminded him that when children express their feelings through tears or act out, they are human. By validating these emotions, I helped him see that he shouldn't let the cries and pain define him, but rather understand the underlying feelings behind those actions.

MODELING EMPATHY

I demonstrated empathy by showing Zephaniah how to respond to his inner child. For instance, when the inner child cried, I suggested he say to himself, "It's okay to cry. It's a way to express what you feel. Your pain is a symbol of how much you care about your baby girl. She meant that much to you. Hold on to that because that is her gift to you." This allowed him to embrace what her impact left with him, emphasizing that tears or frustrations did not define them.

TENDING TO THE CHILD THROUGH THE DAD

I made it a point to hug Zephaniah every chance I got, assuring him that he knew I loved him. At first, some discomfort surfaced, but I could tell it was making a difference when he started saying, "I love you too, Charles." The key is consistently demonstrating love for the child within and suggesting that perhaps that inner child has not received enough love. Often, the smallest and most consistent gestures make all the difference in the world.

CREATING A SAFE SPACE

I advised Zephaniah to create a home environment where emotions were welcomed. I encouraged discussions around feelings, emphasizing that he could share his highs and lows without fear of being labeled or misunderstood. This open dialogue fostered stronger bonds, allowing all to express themselves freely.

ENCOURAGING REFLECTION

When Zephaniah experienced moments of sadness or frustration from his past, I prompted him to reflect on those feelings and share them unapologetically.

SETTING AN EXAMPLE

Finally, I emphasized that Zephaniah's journey of healing and growth was a powerful example for his other children. By openly discussing his emotions and demonstrating resilience, he taught them that it is okay to feel and that those feelings do not define them. They learned to appreciate themselves and others as multifaceted human beings.

Through learning how to nurture his healing, Zephaniah gained insight into how to promote healing for his children, including learning to let go and forgive, both the circumstances around his daughter's death and also the harmful ways in which he had responded. He embraced the idea that we are all human, deserving of understanding and love, regardless of our struggles. This newfound perspective strengthened their family ties and instilled a sense of safety and respect for feelings within their home.

Then there's Darnell, another father who learned to forgive both his father, who hadn't shown love to him as a child, and himself, for believing that his identity somehow made him unable to be a good dad.

At forty-six, Darnell was a dad striving to embrace his identity, navigating the complex intersections of being a gay man and a father. His heart was a labyrinth of emotions, ensnared by guilt and shame for not being more present in his child's life. Darnell's feelings were intensified by the fears that his child might not accept him for who he was.

"What brings you here today, Darnell?" I asked during our first meeting in my office.

"I don't know where to start," he began, his voice trembling. "A part of me wants to know who my father was. Why wasn't he there for me?"

A deep ache surfaced as he recalled the moments of his childhood: the day he first realized he was different, the sting of societal labels attached to his identity, and the relentless thoughts that echoed in his mind.

He continued, "I'm in my mid-forties, and I still want to know about him, where he was, why he wasn't in my life."

In each counseling session, I make it my job to confront any statement that suggests a dad sees himself as unworthy by highlighting the amazing person I see in front of me. Whenever Darnell expressed self-doubt or shame, I reminded him of his strength, his resilience, and the love he fostered for his children as their dad.

Forgiveness became our recurring theme.

"Darnell," I gently reminded him, "you have nothing to forgive yourself for when it comes to who you love or who you choose to be. But you must forgive yourself for the shame that binds you. Let go of believing you're unworthy just because of your sexuality or past struggles with addiction."

Darnell nodded slowly, understanding, but still grappling with the weight of his feelings.

"Sometimes, it's hard to believe that I deserve love," he admitted, his voice cracking. "I feel like I'm not good enough for anyone, not even for my child."

I could see Darnell wanted to forgive himself for his past mistakes and for the mistaken belief that he was somehow less worthy of being a good dad because of his sexual orientation, but it would take work to help him get there. To make the path a bit easier, I broke his journey down into concrete steps.

UNDERSTANDING THE DAMAGE

First, we identified the root cause of his pain by locating specific acts and imagining the scenarios that had instilled blame within him.

SHIFTING THE BLAME

Then we focused on transferring the blame from Darnell to its rightful place, recognizing external factors that were beyond his control. Darnell didn't need to beat himself up for who he was. If society couldn't accept him, that was society's problem, not his own. This step was crucial in allowing Darnell to see that the pain inflicted was not a reflection of his worth.

ADDRESSING SURFACING PAIN

We established a plan to remain conscious of when remnants of that pain resurfaced, addressing them with care. We alluded to this pain as cries from his inner child, acknowledging past trauma as part of his journey. I encouraged Darnell to listen to his inner child, to be gentle and kind with them, and to remember his angels when times got tough.

———

Darnell and I executed this plan diligently, and with each session, he grew closer to recognizing the gift he truly was. In doing so, he began to forgive himself for treating himself as if he were anything less than that gift. Once he was able to forgive himself, he could extend that forgiveness to his own father, acknowledging that his father had faced his own challenges that prevented him from being present—just as he had.

Contextualizing the pain made it easier for Darnell to practice forgiveness. Through tears and laughter, through breakthroughs and setbacks, he embraced the path before him. In reflecting on his journey, he smiled through his tears. "I'm starting to understand that being in my child's life doesn't mean I have to abandon who I am. It means showing up fully, just as I am."

And in that realization, I saw not just a father finding his way, but a man learning to love himself—an embodiment of hope for all those who find themselves in similar shoes, grappling with the complexities of identity, belonging, and unconditional love.

There are many ways to express forgiveness. Sometimes an act of forgiveness is explicit and clear. The person who is forgiving might tell the person who harmed them that they are forgiven, thus releasing them from whatever harmful action they committed. This kind of forgiveness allows the person who caused harm to move on, and it also allows the person offering forgiveness the opportunity to free themselves from a resentful attitude and perhaps even begin the process of healing.

There are also implicit signs of forgiveness, where expressions of forgiveness might at first glance feel entirely absent but, upon closer inspection, are undoubtedly present. Perhaps it's a kind gesture after a fight, or even something as simple as treating someone the way they wish to be treated, even if their past actions suggest they don't necessarily deserve that kind of respect.

But forgiveness, even if difficult, includes many benefits. Expressing forgiveness replaces the possibility of an agonizing spiral with a positive intention and action. Engaging in forgiveness is equivalent to gaining a sense of power and self-protection from the victimization of the act that occurred.

That doesn't mean it's easy, and there are more than a few barriers when it comes to forgiving someone. Through my work as a therapist, I've learned that one common and significant barrier to forgiveness is the inability to tolerate vulnerability. Being unable to sit with vulnerability makes it difficult to forgive when we feel like we've been wronged or treated unfairly. We also find it difficult to forgive when we think our forgiveness shows mercy to someone who does not deserve it. Sometimes, we feel that to forgive is to release our hold on the role of the victim, and some of us are not ready or prepared to do that.

Implicit and explicit expressions of forgiveness cannot entirely rid someone of their painful memories. But one of the values of forgiveness is that it gives agency back to the person offering forgiveness. They can decide how they want to show forgiveness. That is, forgiveness can only be understood and defined by the person who chooses to use it in their own life. The importance of being open to different ways of expressing forgiveness, while considering your situation and level of agony, is essential. When it comes to forgiveness, your choice in how to show it matters most.

Forgiveness is letting go of someone else's choice. I have found that the first step in forgiving is identifying the choices that have led to us feeling a sense of harm. The question we must ask ourselves is, Whose choices are in the room with us?

Whenever I think about my inner child, I recognize that I'm constantly confronting choices that I didn't make and that have nothing to do with me. I've found that writing down all the choices that sit with me has been helpful in differentiating whose choices are motivating my thoughts and actions.

Take my father's decision to decrease his visits to me, especially juxtaposed against the love my father and mother continue to have for one another. For years, I beat myself up about my dad's absence, certain that I was the reason he wasn't around. But that was his choice, not mine. Still, I was angry and hurt about his decision, which felt like a cut that bled into how I viewed my mother's choice to continue her relationship with my father. How could she love a man who had hurt me? I have spent years attempting to understand their relationship and how it has become a source of power for both of them. But that's their choice, not mine.

That realization alone didn't immediately lessen what was a constant fight within me to make sense of these choices. It's been draining. It's taken me a long time, but I've learned the importance of the second step of forgiveness: We must not attempt to make sense of choices we will never understand. Separating yourself from the choices of others requires clearly identifying the choices in the room and remaining aware of them so they don't become your identity. That's crucial to the act of forgiveness.

Sometimes when we're angry at someone, we fight against seeing in that person any sense of humanity. But that can be dangerous, because that kind of resentment can lead to us forfeiting the ability to see the humanity in ourselves. Holding on to anger about someone else's choices ultimately ends up harming ourselves.

Even though I know all about the theories of forgiveness, it hasn't always been easy to incorporate them into my own life. After all, knowing how something as complex as forgiveness should work and trying to integrate it into the messiness of life are two different things. But even adjusting our mindset about our past circumstances, particularly when it comes to trying to understand how another person's actions affect us, can be a powerful step toward healing.

Here's an example. Right as Samantha was experiencing contractions before the birth of our son, Clayton, my mother arrived in Boston for a visit. She had brought with her a collection of photos from my earliest years, my "baby book." As I flipped through the photos, a couple of them caught my eye.

In one, I'm a newborn and my father is holding me. In another, he's assembling my crib. I've spent a long time thinking about my father, and how little he must have thought of me since he wasn't around. But as I prepared for the birth of my own son, these images made me view myself in new ways. Seeing those photos produced a flood of emotions. I was heartened that my dad had been there when I was born, but also angry that those tender moments weren't enough to keep him around in my life. And strangely enough, the photos offered another moment of validation for the child within me. They confirmed that his father had always loved him, even when the world got the best of my father and he wasn't around.

I know that a few old photos can't undo the decades of complicated emotions I've endured because of my father's choices. The reality is that I will never be able to heal completely the wounds that continue to fester, causing difficulty for me to feel like I belong. Even when those who care about me and love me express this, I still sometimes find it difficult to believe.

But by grappling with my feelings, by working on forgiveness, I can choose to respond to my wounds differently, by speaking to the pain so it does not burden my children and those who depend on me. Moments of humanity can be gifts of validation for the children we once were and who continue to reside within us.

I've come to see forgiveness not as a single act, but as a journey, one that continuously requires us to find ways to speak to the pain of our child within. These conversations will look different. Maybe it's a conversation with a loved one, an affirmation from a friend, a visit to a place where you once felt safe and protected. Or maybe it's a photo of a man you wish you knew better, holding you, showing you love, that immediately brings you back to where you were as a child, free and unbothered by the world's complexities.

Sometimes feelings of danger will prompt us to step back from the process of forgiveness. For me, I struggle with forgiveness when my inner child feels frightened or unsafe. Moments when I feel unloved, abandoned, or forgotten make it difficult for me to engage, and I tend to withdraw or become angry. As parents, we must identify those moments and store them somewhere safely outside of our minds. Otherwise, we risk passing on that trauma to those we love.

One barrier to forgiveness is often the proximity to that moment when you felt harmed but have not been able to overcome. If enough time has gone by, perhaps offering forgiveness becomes easier. Though not always. The danger alarm remains stored in our minds even when the physical location is different, even if many years have gone by.

The child within us carries everything. But by seeking to understand the elements that comprise moments when forgiveness feels far off, we can make sure that they don't blindside us. An exercise I sometimes ask of the men I work with is to write a letter to themselves that explicitly states the location where they experienced a painful moment, a description of what happened, a list of the individuals involved, and an exploration of the emotions they felt during that experience. If a person has experienced many painful events, I suggest they write a separate letter for each one. Then I encourage them to store these letters somewhere safe.

Truly forgiving another person must include a recognition that forgiveness is not about that person. Instead, it's about our willingness to let go of anything that played a role in creating those moments when we didn't feel safe or loved, so that we can focus on the lessons connected to that painful experience.

I am not suggesting that to forgive, one must forget what occurred and not hold the person accountable for the act. That's also true even if we are the person who needs to be held accountable to ourselves. Those painful moments ruptured us and then became a revolving door. We run the risk of walking through that door at any time, so it's important to understand and grapple with those painful moments, lest we end up trapped in that door. Although the effects of those moments will remain with us, we can reduce their impact by clearly shedding light on our moments. It's necessary.

When we relive pain from past experiences, it's easy to think that it will be unpleasant. And often it will be. But those moments can also be a gift, worth examining with curiosity.

———

When I was younger, my elders often reminded me that there are two sides to a coin. During moments of pain, it can be difficult to see the other side of the coin, but it's still there. The feelings that the pain brought became a norm and a necessity for my survival. The gift of spending time with those painful moments was that they no longer controlled my life.

Over the years, I've learned to have a better handle on my emotions, and I've discovered a deeper sense of how I can control those painful moments when they arise. But that doesn't mean it's easy. Often, when I'm visiting home, places from my childhood, it feels like it's nothing more than the place where my most painful memories are stored. But when I'm willing to put in the work of reimagining the scene around me, I'm able to see that home is also a place where I experienced other moments, when I felt safe and loved. I try to remind my inner child of those moments, too. Plus, when I'm with Samantha and our two kids, it's easier to remember that I'm no longer the child I was back then.

Forgiveness is a dance. I remind the men I work with that even if they are in the thick of pain and can't imagine a way to offer forgiveness, to others or to themselves, they will get there someday. They can use their pain and anger today to make a difference tomorrow. They will eventually find the ability to let go.

Revisiting the choices present with us in the room, identifying the nature of our interior cries, and understanding behavior from those moments of pain—that can all lead to discovering opportunities to use that pain in a more productive way. We don't have to be perfect, nor rid ourselves of all the moments that don't feel good. But we can learn to live with those moments. When we do, we become one step closer to forgiving.

Back in Georgia, all those years ago, when I met my father and my uncles, I told my dad that I forgave him. As he drove away, I realized that my words were merely aspirational, that even though I wanted so badly to forgive him, so that I could begin to heal, I wasn't ready then.

Today, things are different. I'm still on a journey of forgiveness and I realize that I can't manifest the destination into being. I have to trust that the journey itself will be healing, and that by focusing on forgiveness, it may someday be attainable. If not for my father, perhaps for me.

Lesson: What you thought you knew is not always accurate. Whenever students create stories about themselves with limited information, inaccuracies are inevitable. It's crucial to identify these gaps to prevent them from distorting the narrative.

12. MY FIRST TIME

I magine stepping into a new position at a job without knowing what the position entailed. No one told you your new role, how it works, or what's expected of you. That's what it's like becoming a parent for the first time. It's well documented that expectant moms, especially women of color, need better access to resources about becoming good parents. And though it's less talked about, expectant dads face an equally damaging deficit when it comes to resources available to help them with this major life event.

My own journey began back in 2012, when Samantha and I were in our mid-twenties and about to take on major life changes. I proposed, she said yes, and though we hadn't lived together yet and were unsure about how it would work, we were both ready to commit to each other and begin our lives anew.

About a year after the wedding, Samantha wasn't feeling well, complaining of cramps and discomfort.

"I think we should go to the doctor," she told me.

We found the closest urgent care clinic. The medical team

ran a series of tests and then a doctor came into the room. Samantha was sitting on the exam table and I was next to her, in a chair. The doctor looked at Samantha, never acknowledging me at all.

"You're pregnant," the doctor said, solely to Samantha.

I can't say I remember much of what happened next, but I'll never forget how I felt. The doctor never looked me in the eye, never asked if I had any questions, never even glanced in my direction. I felt invisible, as if this news wouldn't affect me at all.

Still, I comforted Samantha, who seemed as shocked as I was. I don't think I told her at the time, but I was terrified.

Wow, I'm going to have a baby, I thought to myself. *Oh my God, I'm going to have a baby!*

I'm sure most people feel a rush of emotions when they learn that they will become parents for the first time. I was shocked, excited, and happy—but also devastated. I didn't have a relationship with my father. I spent most of my free time helping men learn how to be good fathers. And yet I knew that, deep down, I had no idea how I would be as a father. My mind went to dark places, fearful that I would pass on my own trauma to my child, that the cycle would continue. Would I fail this little baby even before he or she was born?

At that point in my life, I lacked a strong network of young fathers to whom I could turn for advice. The men I did approach took a decidedly old-school approach when it came to preparing for fatherhood. One told me that the only resource I needed was the Bible, a book that remains important to me, but one that doesn't offer much by way of modern parenting advice. Another father told me to make sure I was okay, otherwise I wouldn't be able to care for Samantha or the baby. Good advice, but how did I make sure I was okay?

On top of being pregnant, we were both dealing with the stress of not having enough money. I was busy trying to build Fathers' UpLift and Samantha was finishing her graduate program at Boston College. The compound stress led to lots of fights, which felt so significant at the time but in reality were driven by both of us feeling scared and insecure about our futures. For me, the depression, anxiety, self-doubt, and shame built up because I felt like I had no one to talk to about my emotions. This led to bickering with Samantha, who subsequently didn't feel like she could rely on me to help her process her own emotions because I was struggling with my own. At one point, I feared we were on the verge of divorce, an outcome neither of us wanted, but which seemed inevitable.

In a clumsy attempt to explain to Samantha what I was feeling, I told her one day that I felt "mentally pregnant." I explained my mood swings, the roller coaster of being excited about a baby and terrified that I'd let that baby down. I was stressed out, gaining weight, and my emotions were all over the place.

"I don't know what the hell is going on with me," I told Samantha. "I feel like the third wheel in this situation."

Samantha, very much both mentally and physically pregnant, didn't exactly appreciate the comparison. When you're dealing with the physical and emotional discomfort of carrying a baby, I suppose it makes sense that you don't want to hear your partner compare their uncertainty to your own physical challenges. Once again, I was trying to explain my emotions, but tripping over my own two feet in the process.

The weeks went by, the fights continued, but then the moment we'd been waiting for arrived.

On the way to the hospital, our mutual stress manifested in more fighting, but I think deep down we knew we would both be there for each other. We checked in to the labor and delivery floor, were shown to our room, and I played some soft background music to try to help ease some of Samantha's pain. A nurse entered the room to check on Samantha and make sure she was all right. Everything was proceeding according to plan, but I still felt like I had no one to help me process my anxieties.

Every once in a while, with Samantha's blessing, I'd leave the room and wander the Brigham and Women's Hospital hallways. I can still trace the route to this day. Right. Left. Left. This would take me past the reception area, and I remember muttering to no one in particular during one of these walks, "This is crazy! I can't take this."

"I know, baby, it's gonna be okay," I heard a voice say from the reception area.

They were the first words of reassurance I had heard from someone in weeks. A stranger, a receptionist on a busy labor and delivery ward, and a godsend to me.

Later, during another bout of anxiety, I took another walk.

"Baby, it's gonna be okay, you're gonna make it through."

This same woman didn't know me or Samantha, she didn't know my backstory or the stress I was facing, but she took a second to reassure me that things would indeed be okay. She didn't know that I wasn't getting that support from Samantha or from my family or from my colleagues. While Samantha, thankfully, had a team of doctors and nurses looking out for her, and the baby had a pediatrician lined up to care for him, I felt very much on my own. Those few seconds with that receptionist that night meant the world to me.

Back in the hospital room, Clayton was ready to be born.

Everything seemed to be progressing well, when all of a sudden, commotion and chaos erupted. The doctor on hand to help with delivery noticed something was wrong and saw that Clayton's shoulder was stuck. Recognizing the danger, the doctor jumped into action. I saw her lower her shoulder, drop down, and perform some kind of wrestling-like maneuver that I suppose was aimed at helping the baby get out and saving Samantha's life.

"Oh shit!" I yelled as my son entered the world. Then I almost fainted.

A couple of hours later, once Clayton had returned from the neonatal ICU, Samantha was able to hold him and get that all-important skin-to-skin contact. I was overcome with emotion. I had been so worried about becoming a father, but the time for worry was over. I had a baby who was dependent on me. I had to step up. I had to be present.

In the weeks that followed, Samantha, Clayton, and I were surrounded by love. Our family, friends, and colleagues bought clothes and groceries. Samantha's mom traveled up from New York to watch Clayton when we needed a break. Samantha became a couponing queen, helping to stretch our already thin budget ever further. And we both did our best to be kinder to ourselves, admitting that we didn't know what we didn't know and that even still, it would all work out.

Meeting with the fathers whose group I was facilitating proved to be a lifeline during these stressful days. I was helping them process their experiences, and they were also listening to me share my own fears and anxieties. And since they often had a lot more experience when it came to fatherhood, they were able to offer some advice and guidance, which turned out to be a lot more practical and insightful than some of the advice I had received during Samantha's pregnancy.

My experience leading up to Clayton's birth had been scary,

stressful, and fraught for our marriage. Once Clayton was born, there was a whole new set of issues to deal with, but I never forgot how unprepared I had been when it came to imagining my new life as a dad. I can easily picture things turning out differently. Overcome with self-doubt and shame, fighting constantly with Samantha, stressed about money, perhaps I might have justified to myself that Samantha and our son would be better off if I simply left. She had her mother, after all, and what was I contributing besides unneeded worry?

It's nothing short of a miracle that I chose a different path. But miracles can't be counted on for everyone.

Before Clayton was born, as I wrestled with the question of what it means to be a provider and protector, I was also figuring out why I was experiencing sleepless nights, self-doubt, fear, and phases of depression. I needed guidance, research I could read, a chart to follow—but no one in my corner seemed equipped to help me understand what I felt. I needed more diversity in the information that's given to new fathers. The process I was experiencing had no form; it was just a series of feelings with no order, and I couldn't find helpful information anywhere. That's true for countless fathers.

Anyone who's been through the process of becoming a new father, and anyone who's accompanied a man who has gone through this, knows well that something is going on with them, even if it's difficult to describe. Still, medical and psychological professionals have yet to figure out what exactly is happening during this critical transition.

Men face countless messages each day that hammer home the myth that to express what we're feeling is a sign of weakness. And any perception of weakness is a ding on our masculinity. This means many men are reluctant to ask for help. And the consequences can be disastrous.

In the realm of pregnancy discourse, maternal health often takes center stage, overshadowing the nuanced experiences of fathers. This is especially pronounced within diverse communities in the United States, where significant disparities in pregnancy outcomes exist. According to the Centers for Disease Control and Prevention, African American and Black women are three times more likely to face fatal complications during pregnancy compared to their white counterparts. They also grapple with higher incidences of preterm births and stillbirths, exacerbating the stresses surrounding pregnancy.[25]

At the same time, the emotional and psychological journeys of expectant fathers remain under-explored. Research indicates that fathers often experience feelings akin to being sidelined—aware of their partner's struggles yet grappling with their own moodiness, anxiety, and isolation. These experiences are compounded by the societal expectation to be the primary provider, introducing further layers of stress and pressure.

For African American and Black fathers, these complexities may be intensified by cultural and systemic factors that affect their support systems and mental health. Understanding their unique experiences is crucial for their well-being and the overall health of families and communities. This exploration helps unveil the often-overlooked narratives of fathers during pregnancy, highlighting how their perceptions and experiences can influence maternal health outcomes and family dynamics.

By delving into the realities faced by these fathers, we can foster a more inclusive understanding of pregnancy that encompasses the emotional landscapes of all involved, ultimately contributing to healthier and more supportive environments for mothers and their children. As I reflect on some of the dads I have encountered in my work, many examples remain a part of me.

Once a boy growing up in the heart of the South, Jonathan spent his formative years shaped by a childhood that weighed heavily on his spirit into adulthood. Watching his mother toil tirelessly to provide for him, he saw his father fade into absence, a development that cultivated a profound longing within Jonathan. At the time, Jonathan didn't recognize a deep-rooted desire to break the cycle, but he did recognize a painful realization that other families felt more whole than his own. Each day, as he watched his friends' fathers, men who dropped them off at school with a kiss on the forehead, he envisioned a different future for himself, especially for his future children.

"I am not going to put my daughter through the things that I went through," he often vowed to himself while waiting for her arrival.

Even though Jonathan had ideas about the kind of father he didn't want to be, the notion of being a father had always seemed abstract to Jonathan; it was never a topic of discussion among the men he grew up with.

"As men, we were never taught how to be fathers," he reflected later, frustrated that the tradition was being passed on to him even while he was feeling powerless to change it. The unfamiliar terrain was disorienting, and the expectations—to be present, to nurture, to guide—felt like burdens rather than the gifts he knew they should be. However, things began to change when he sought the camaraderie of other fathers. Jonathan found a sense of belonging in the company of men who shared similar stories of struggle and triumph.

Their conversations, filled with laughter and vulnerability, offered insights into the intricacies of fatherhood. Slowly but surely, Jonathan began to realize that parenting was as much about presence as it was about perfection.

Amid this journey of discovery, the emotional scars of his past began to surface. Rather than embracing learning opportunities, Jonathan often found himself retreating into a battle with his unresolved feelings. He was overwhelmed by the weight of his past, caught in patterns of avoidance that had haunted him for years. Important moments, like attending prenatal appointments or reading to his unborn daughter, felt like distant obligations rather than acts of love.

"I was lost," he admitted, grappling with the silent struggle. However, with each shared story and supportive nod from his newfound father friends, he began reconnecting with his vision of parenthood. The turning point came one evening as he stood in the nursery, a book in hand, realizing that reading to his baby in the womb was not just an obligation but a cherished opportunity to bond. It ignited a spark within him, a promise that he would create a different reality for those babies he was privileged to nurture.

Jonathan eventually committed to showing up, to being emotionally present, to ensure that his daughter never felt the absence of a father, a memory that still haunted him.

As the days turned into weeks and months, Jonathan transformed from a passive observer of fatherhood into an engaged participant. He embraced the small moments, such as the late-night feedings, the soothing lullabies, and the shared laughter, and he let them strengthen his resolve. He chipped away at the shadows of his childhood, forging a new legacy anchored in love and presence. Through his journey, he learned how to be a father, and he even became a beacon for others navigating the murky waters of fatherhood.

These seemingly simple conversations with other dads and soon-to-be dads connected Jonathan with his emotions and allowed him to redefine his upbringing, turning hurt into hope and isolation into community. Ultimately, Jonathan's journey became a testament to the power of vulnerability, growth, and the relentless pursuit of being the father he always wished he had.

Another first-time dad, Fabian, grew up weaving through life's complexities in a small Southern town, cradled in the warmth of his mother's care. He had always identified as a loving and nurturing individual, and he wore that identity like a badge of honor. His childhood was filled with love and support, particularly from his mother. She infused their home with laughter and resilience, even when questions loomed large, particularly the ever-present question: "Where is my father?"

The grace Fabian's mother exhibited was profound. Throughout her life, she spoke of his father with nothing but kindness, never allowing negativity to seep into her son's consciousness. Because of her, Fabian had a picture of a man who was a stranger yet somehow heroic in his absence. However, as he grew older, the shadows of curiosity deepened into creeping doubts. His father's absence, rather than fading into obscurity, morphed into an insistent echo, whispering uncertainties that reverberated in his mind. Though he had been surrounded by other male figures, like his brother's father and his sister's father, the longing for his own was palpable. The presence of his siblings' fathers never filled the void. In fact, it highlighted the absence, leaving his heart grappling with emotions he couldn't fully articulate.

It was not until he was about to become a father himself that Fabian recognized the clarity of purpose woven into that painful narrative. Determined to establish a new generational legacy, Fabian vowed to be the kind of father he witnessed in others: a father who shows up, who engages, who loves unconditionally. Despite the looming shadows of his childhood, he fought resolutely against the inertia of negativity that threatened to define him. "The absence of a father will not bind me," he reminded himself, anchoring his intentions in love despite the unknown that surrounded him.

But the journey to becoming that kind of father, especially when he lacked an example from his own life, would be challenging.

Balancing work, family, and the weight of expectations sometimes felt overwhelming. There were struggles with self-doubt and moments of uncertainty when he questioned whether he could be the father he aspired to be. Yet through every trial, Fabian kept his focus on presence, reminding himself that the attempt mattered most—the willingness to try, to show up, and to love fiercely. Mistakes were inevitable, but he learned they did not define his ability to father. Instead, each misstep became an opportunity for connection, a moment of honesty to share with his children.

He often mused, "It is not perfection but my effort that will shape them."

Fabian wasn't starting on empty. The memories of his mother's kindness were a guiding light, illuminating his path as he navigated the intricate landscape of fatherhood. As years passed, Fabian grew more steadfast in his resolve, embracing the beauty in the imperfections of life. His father's absence morphed from a painful enigma into a catalyst for love and growth. He became a beacon for his children, offering them the sort of stability and affection that was once a wish and is now a vibrant reality; he also mentored other young men to be the kind of men he had longed for as a child.

Ultimately, Fabian transformed his unanswered questions into powerful affirmations of love and strength. In his heart, he knew that while he might never understand why his father was absent, he was determined to rewrite the narrative of fatherhood. Through his efforts, each loving moment became a testament to a father's love, carved out of his own experiences and bathed in the light of his mother's unwavering influence. Ultimately, he understood that his presence—his heart and soul—would define him as a father.

COMPELLING THEMES DURING PREGNANCY

Both Jonathan and Fabian experienced themes that are common to many new dads, especially men who grew up without a father regularly in their lives. For Jonathan, he worried that his own identity was defined by his father.

"I kept wondering who I am in all this," Jonathan recalled later.

His partner was younger than him, and as the pregnancy progressed, he had more questions than answers. "I can't help but think about my father's interests, particularly his penchant for younger women. Does that somehow shape who I am?"

He paused, searching for clarity amid confusion. "It is like trying to piece together a puzzle without the correct pieces. I never even knew him, and now I'm haunted by thoughts of who he was," he recalled.

Fabian, like many other dads, made a promise to himself—but one he needed help keeping.

"I will not be like my father. I will not repeat the mistakes he made," he told himself.

His voice, though soft, carried a weighty desperation. "His absence, his criticisms, they shadowed my childhood. I just refuse to take that road."

Fabian and Jonathan agreed with the notion that most men see themselves as fathers only after the baby arrives. That's because there isn't good prenatal care for dads. What is expected of new fathers? It's a question lots of dads ask themselves, but like in my own experience, there just aren't many good answers.

I've broken down my answers into two categories. One for those supporting new dads, and the other for new fathers themselves. First, here are some helpful tips for creating the kinds of spaces where expectant fathers will be comfortable showing vulnerability and asking questions. These are the ways I conduct my work at Fathers' UpLift.

VALIDATE

Remembering the importance of fathers in your life is essential. A simple acknowledgment can go a long way in boosting their confidence and reinforcing their caregiver role.

ENGAGE BOTH PARENTS

In today's world, it is too easy for families to drift apart. Emphasizing the significance of both parents working together can create a more supportive environment for everyone involved.

FOSTER A WELCOMING ENVIRONMENT

Create spaces where fathers feel valued and included. Regularly communicating the importance of their role encourages a sense of belonging and purpose within the family dynamic.

ASSESS AND OUTREACH

Ensure the father and his partner feel safe during the pregnancy, recognizing that stress can affect everyone. After establishing the father's involvement, reach out and maintain open lines of communication to provide support.

ACKNOWLEDGE

Use eye contact and positive body language to convey that dads are meant to be present. Comparing their experience to someone being treated for a wound emphasizes that the emotional and physical labor of pregnancy is valid and should not be overlooked. A dad's role is just as critical, even if it is not always visible.

EDUCATE

Recognize that pregnancy comes with challenges, and many parents enter this phase with limited knowledge. Providing accurate information, resources, and support empowers them to understand their roles better and prepares them for the journey ahead. Stress that their involvement begins long before the child's birth, and break down the expectations and responsibilities associated with parenthood.

———

Through these recommendations, new fathers learn to navigate their experiences confidently, fostering healthier family dynamics and ultimately enriching the lives of both parents and children.

Next, here are some ideas I try to instill in new dads. I've used lessons from my own experience becoming a father, and the experiences of new dads like Jonathan and Fabian, to come up with a resource I call Pre-Father Care.

BLESSINGS

First, I remind expectant fathers that what they are about to experience is a blessing—the joyful moments and also the challenges. Those challenges might leave scars, but they often contain beauty as well.

In those early days of caring for Clayton, the idea of walking away from it all crossed my mind. I'm not proud to admit it, but I was under so much pressure and I lacked the tools to figure out how to manage all the stress, so I thought leaving might be best for everyone. Years later, I'm glad I responded differently.

Whenever I face challenges today, when external factors make me feel like I have no control over anything in my life, I remind myself of the beauty of fatherhood, even if it was a bumpy journey early on.

When we're able to find a lesson associated with a scar, that is a gift. If we focus too intensely on how we were wronged, or how stressful the scarring experience was, we risk losing that gift and, with it, we forfeit that gift's ability to help guide us through future challenges.

That's not to say that a person must like or condone an unpleasant, challenging, or stressful experience in order to find value in it, in the form of a lesson. But beauty is ever present. Finding it depends on how deeply we search for it.

STARE AT IT

Sometimes I like to share this parable with new dads. An artist famous for his work experienced a shake in his drawing hand. He didn't know where the tremor originated, so he went to a doctor to get it checked out.

"You'll have this condition for the rest of your life, and you must embrace the shake," the doctor said.

The artist left the doctor's appointment, his head filled with anxiety about his future. But when the artist took pen to paper, to his surprise, his art was even better than before the shake, and he went on to achieve even more success.

The lesson of this story is that it's important to embrace our past and current realities, even if they feel scary or stressful or uncertain. For new parents, that means embracing the chaos while never forgetting their full potential. We can't erase our pasts, but we can look for lessons from what we've endured.

I put so much pressure on myself to be the perfect dad right after Clayton was born, in part because my dad hadn't been around and I didn't want Clayton to have to deal with the same frustrations and disappointments that had tarnished my childhood. But another part of my striving for perfection was a response to the messaging I received about what it means to be a man. I wanted the cash to buy the perfect house. I wanted Clayton to have the hottest toys and access to the best schools. I had to be good at sports, and everything else, so that Clayton would look up to me with respect and admiration. And I had to be the man of the house, whatever that means.

All that self-directed pressure came crashing down one day when Clayton looked up at me and said, "Dad, you are the best dad in the world because . . ."

I wondered where he was going with this. I had worked hard to provide my son the kind of childhood I never had, the experiences that would make him grow into a strong, confident man, one who wasn't weighed down with generational trauma. Would he finish that sentence by recognizing my sacrifices? Pointing to the toys I buy him?

". . . you make the best peanut butter and jelly sandwich."

The best dad in the world, because I make him sandwiches? And that's not even my best sandwich! But Clayton found value in me slopping some peanut butter and jarred jelly onto two slices of bread and calling it a meal.

Why did I find this so startling? Well, for starters, I had built up in my mind all sorts of metrics and traits and skills I needed in order to be a good dad, but Clayton cut through all that and reminded me that it's actually far simpler. He didn't care about how much money I made. He didn't care about the house that he lived in. He didn't even seem to care about the quality of the toys I purchased for him. He just wanted to thank me for being present to make a sandwich.

It took me a long time to realize that my son wanted something much different from perfection. He wanted my time.

CARE FOR OURSELVES

Men often hear unrealistic messages about how we should live our lives, and a lot of times we don't feel like we are measuring up. But the way we respond internally to external messages or circumstances can be the difference between succeeding and failing.

People sometimes tell me that they're struck by my seemingly relentless optimism. When I'm leading groups of men for our check-in sessions, I adopt a can-do coaching attitude. "Game time!" is a constant refrain. I want to help men find the confidence they need to achieve their fatherhood goals, despite some exceedingly challenging pasts. I apply the same attitude in my own life. I tell myself that I can do anything if I put my mind to it. Whenever memories from the past threaten my goals, I acknowledge those feelings but then move on.

No, I didn't like how that felt, but that bad feeling won't define me. Yes, I'm angry, but I'll use that anger as a motivation to do something better. I may not have been as present in my children's lives as I'd like to have been over the past few months, but guess what? Today is a new day, and I can be a better father.

Sometimes, our response to uncomfortable feelings can get in our way. But it's important to remember that the feelings themselves aren't the issue; it's natural to experience a range of emotions. But our responses to those feelings are key. In situations in which you feel like your feelings are taking control, ask yourself, "Will my response allow me to be here another day to see my children grow?" If your answer is no, you must think strategically about how you can respond to the situation in a different way. Continue to ask yourself this question during challenging times. For new fathers, there will be many such times. And taking a moment to ask this question can help you power through them.

A helpful exercise I teach the men I work with is developing an affirmation statement, something simple that they can remember in times of crisis. My own reminder is simple: *Charles, you're unique. You can do anything you put your mind to. And whatever has happened to you that you don't like, use it as a lesson to move forward, because that's what great people do: They hurt, they look for a lesson, and they apply it.* Practicing self-affirmations is an opportunity to remind yourself, and your inner child, that you are in control, regardless of what the world is telling you.

THE FATHER OF THE MAN

There is a saying that the inner child will always be the father of the man. Within us, there's a child who has had his own experiences, and he shapes how the man lives his own life.

For men who are about to become fathers, it's essential that they think critically about how they treat their inner child. Are you judgmental? If you are, you need to stop. Are you caring? If you mess up this time, do you try to reassure your inner child that you'll get it next time?

Lots of men tend to treat ourselves the same way we were treated as children. That can be great if you had a pleasant, supportive, and nurturing childhood. But what if you didn't?

I tell men to think of some practices that they adopted from those who parented them when they were children, and consider how those practices continue to affect how they treat themselves today. If they grew up in a household where being a child was difficult and their parents were harsh, on their backs most of the time and judgmental about their choices, maybe they've brought some of those same practices into their self-parenting. It's important to reflect on this reality when preparing to be a new parent, because the way you parent your inner child is probably going to be reflected in how you parent your physical child. You cannot be a parent to another person if you cannot parent yourself.

FORGIVENESS IS KEY

New fathers must remember that forgiveness is essential, whether directed at others or themselves.

Everyone is imperfect. Friends and even our family members will hurt us, sometimes intentionally but more often accidentally, and we again are faced with a choice: Do we focus on the pain caused by the offense or do we strive for forgiveness?

We do not have to stay hostage to our own actions or even other people's actions. So yes, it's important to forgive others, but it's also important to forgive yourself. The fallout of refusing to forgive others mirrors what might happen if we refuse to forgive ourselves. We'll be stuck, unable to move forward.

The only thing that we can control is how we free ourselves from the pain that comes from being wronged. If men are unable to forgive others or forgive themselves, they will limit their growth, and their relationships with their children may suffer. Forgiveness might feel like something being offered to another person, and in some instances, we might feel as if the person who harmed us doesn't deserve forgiveness. But withholding forgiveness often harms us more than it hurts them. And when we are responsible for a child, our inability to forgive may even be passed on to another generation.

TRANSFORMATION IS A PROCESS

Growth can be painful, but you can get through it. I know that because it happened for me.

In the first few years of Clayton's life, I became preoccupied with getting it right. An obsession with perfection can be harmful, but in my parenting journey, there was one component of wanting to get it right that took time to accept but ultimately proved to be a blessing: I learned to learn from my mistakes.

At first, I wasn't open to seeing where I came up short. I wanted to fix my errors quickly, sometimes thinking that if I could right the wrongs fast enough, it would almost be like they had never happened. I just had to get them right the first time. When I cooked a new recipe, it had to be perfect the first time for me to feel like I was doing a good job taking care of my family. Of course, getting something right the very first time is rare. But it took me a while to accept that. This is common for a lot of new dads. It took some time, but I've learned it's also okay if you don't get it right the first time, the second time, or the third time—because every attempt is an opportunity for growth. How would learning occur if everything we did was done perfectly the first time? Sometimes, you might get it right the first time, or you may never get it exactly right, but that's okay. It's all about growth. I tell new fathers that perfection isn't the point. Learning from our attempts at perfection is far more important.

FROM HELPLESSNESS TO POWER

Human beings have moments of weakness. We're imperfect. We need to own that. The exhaustion I felt from trying to be strong all the time actually made me weak. I didn't realize I needed to stop thinking that way until I was exhausted and at my lowest.

When it all got to be too much, I would have to stop and say to myself, "Charles, you know what? You are killing yourself, trying to be everything for everybody. It is not your responsibility to be strong all the time. It is not your responsibility to be everything to everybody. Be what you need to be for you."

I got tired of feeling exhausted. I understood that I had to change the unrealistic thought pattern. I realized that if I always focused on trying to be strong, I would always feel depleted. You can't pour from an empty cup.

Before Clayton was born, I knew I wanted to be a present father. It took a little while longer for me to learn that I wouldn't be present if I was always trying to be strong. That realization changed me.

WHAT WE LEAVE BEHIND

As I prepared to become a father myself, I thought of the legacy I wanted to leave my son. I wanted to convey to him that pain is a gift in disguise that, if he uses it the right way, could change generations. My pain, channeled into my life's work, has helped men turn their lives around and be present in the lives of their children. I wouldn't call this a silver lining—I still wish my dad had been present in my life—but I took the legacies I inherited and used them to help others.

I tell new dads to always remember their legacy. It won't be defined by the car you drive, where you live, or what you purchase. Instead, it will be determined by the memories you create, the lessons you leave behind, and the way you make your loved ones feel. Make those the priority. Legacies are created over a lifetime. There isn't a single dramatic moment, but a series of choices we make each day.

THE FATHER I WANT TO BE

What happens in our pasts affects us in ways that aren't always readily evident, starting with our relationship with the fathers in our lives. My father shaped my life, even though he wasn't really there. Some fathers are physically present, but emotionally absent. Others try their best, but come up short. I've heard from lots of men who say they want to be good dads, but who also fear turning into their own fathers. Others tell me they had excellent fathers, but worry they can't measure up to their dads.

I remind new fathers that they have the power to chart whatever fatherhood course they want for their children. Past experiences will undoubtedly shape their approach to fatherhood, but they shouldn't feel beholden to the past. And of course, present realities will also influence their fatherhood experiences. But one thing is key: Remain aware of how your experiences, past and present, shape your emotions.

What must you do to stay in control and maintain the presence of the father you want to be to your children? If you did have a father or a father figure in your life who was a positive influence, use them as your North Star. Rely on them as one of your angels.

When I think back to the earliest days of Clayton's life, I can't believe I made it through at all. There weren't many resources to help me understand just how drastically my life was about to change or to help prepare me for the many challenges that awaited Samantha and me. With too little sleep, and way too much chaos, I felt like my life was spinning out of control. That's why I urge new fathers to remember that we are the authors of our own stories. We shape ourselves into the kinds of fathers we want to be by stepping back from the challenges we face and taking control of our emotions. Change is possible; it helps us grow. Patience is key. Regardless of our pasts, we can be the kinds of fathers we want for our kids.

Six years after Clayton arrived, our daughter, SaMya, was born. Samantha and I were both more mature, our work was more stable, and we had been through the birth of a child once already. So in many ways, we were both much more prepared for the challenges and joys that awaited us. But that didn't mean it was easy.

SaMya was born in the early, frightening days of the pandemic, right around the time that protesters across the country marched against police brutality. The murder of George Floyd had sparked an all-too-rare moment of national self-reflection about how police officers interact with people of color, particularly Black men. By that point, I had been diagnosed with general anxiety disorder, and the disturbing images flooding social media depicting violence against Black people at the hands of police prompted a wave of stress and worry. I wondered what we were thinking in deciding to bring another child into this world. I already worried about Clayton and how the world would perceive him.

My anxiety about racism and the isolation of the pandemic both took their toll, but by being able to draw on lessons from Clayton's birth, Samantha and I prepared ourselves for SaMya's.

Samantha's labor was mostly smooth, and SaMya came out fist-first, ready to take on the world. Whereas with Clayton I felt terrified, afraid, and unprepared, with SaMya, Samantha and I were ready. Our family would be present for one another.

> **Lesson:** There is no such thing as perfection. We should continuously challenge any notion or belief that implies otherwise. Our legacy is defined not by how flawless we are but by how we navigate through challenges and adversity. Identifying the challenge and welcoming it into the classroom makes a difference.

13. HELPING MEN HEAL

Loss is a common theme in my work with new dads, and it's something that we work hard to address. Research reveals that individuals begin grieving loss even before someone or something is gone. This is known as anticipatory grief or mourning. And it exists for more than just physical death. Loss can include the end of a relationship, or a sustained or permanent absence due to unfortunate life events. It can also include changes like losing a community after moving to a new city or leaving a job. Even in otherwise joyful moments, such as having a child, there might be a feeling of loss when the new parent thinks about giving up his or her leisurely weekends with friends. That's why it's especially important to ask expectant dads their feelings about what they might expect to lose once the baby arrives.

Anticipatory grief is a phenomenon that is well-documented when it comes to discussing life-threatening illnesses. But what about other kinds of loss? I've been curious how anticipatory grief affects familial situations, such as when children long to be close to an absent parent or when relationships are fragmented in some form.

In a popular model of grief, there are five stages that describe the process individuals experience after a loss: denial, bargaining, depression, anger, and acceptance. Or put another way, when someone is dealing with loss, it's common for their emotional reactions to include an overwhelming feeling that the world is unbearable due to that loss. I know firsthand what that feels like, because I experienced anticipatory grief in mourning the loss of a relationship with my father.

Growing up, I often questioned the point of my existence, because I couldn't understand my father's absence. The Austrian psychiatrist Victor Frankl studied how human beings find meaning in life, and as I learned about his work, I began to ask myself, "What's my purpose?" Discerning why we exist, our purpose in life, can be a form of healing. It's a lifelong journey, one that Frankl dubbed "logotherapy." For Frankl, the transformative nature of loss can play an important role in one's ability to find meaning even in the midst of suffering and loss.

I'd argue that we are all aggressively searching for meaning. In my case, my response to suffering changed periodically. I viewed the unknown whereabouts of my father as an evil byproduct of this life, one that I blamed myself for in the absence of a logical explanation for his departure. I lacked direction and couldn't understand my purpose, because the loss of a relationship with my father made me feel like I couldn't possibly be of any value to anyone else. But ultimately, with time and understanding, I utilized my experiences with anticipatory grief to find a purpose that is larger than myself—helping other men be good dads.

Employing painful experiences to find meaning in one's life

can take place in a few different ways. First, someone might channel their pain into the creation of a piece of work or a good deed. Next, they might experience something or encounter someone as a result of trying to heal from their pain. Finally, they may adapt their attitudes toward unavoidable suffering, thus steeling themselves against future painful events.

For me, I took the negative experience I had with my father's absence and developed a passion for supporting fathers to help them remain positively engaged in their children's lives using therapy, love, and unconditional regard. I don't want others to experience the kind of anticipatory grief I've endured because of my father's absence. But I take comfort in knowing that I've been able to channel that grief into something positive, an experience that continues to bring me meaning and purpose.

Loss and grief are common in the meetings I have with men at Fathers' UpLift, and I vividly remember the first group session I conducted. It was a turning point in my journey with fathers seeking healing. One man stood out among the dozen or so guys present that night, not just because of his story but because of the light he carried in his presence.

Travis smiled brightly as he introduced himself, revealing that he and his son, Deion, were staying at the shelter just across the street. Travis explained that while things were rough now, he kept on fighting to make his circumstances better, because he knew his son deserved a better life.

"He keeps me moving forward, because I have to be here for him to make sure he's okay," he said of his son. "I love him and will do everything I can to make sure he's all right. I live for him."

Despite the situation, Travis was still able to smile and allow for the possibility that his situation would be uplifted. The entire group seemed to feel inspiration from Travis's optimism. His words resonated deeply, a reminder of what it meant to strive for strength amid adversity. I couldn't help but admire the way he framed his struggles with optimism. I posed a question.

"You're here with a smile on your face, and you're staying at a shelter across the street," I said. "Man, you stand here before us with an encouraging word and smile despite what you're going through. I admire that about you. What is it that allows you to smile with your son by your side, despite these challenges?"

Travis paused for a few moments to consider my question.

"My son looks up to me, and as his dad, I have a choice every day," he said. "I can let our situation define us, or I can create a joyful experience for him, despite the struggles. I want him to know that no matter what happens, we will be okay. He deserves to see the world through a lens of hope, not despair. So, I smile because I'm grateful for the time we have together, regardless of where we are. It's the little moments that matter most."

After hearing the touching story, I asked the men what they thought.

"We sometimes think that our kids may want money all the time and other things that we may or may not be able to provide," one man said. "What is most important is our presence in their lives. Regardless of what we may be going through, we have to continue to be present in their lives despite the challenges."

Travis could have given in to anticipatory loss, the idea that he would lose the opportunity to give his son a good life, and maybe grief would accompany that reality. But he instead focused on what he could do to prevent that loss, and his optimism helped carry him through his present difficulties.

There was also Deron, whose life seemed to be defined by the love he had for his son, Roy—and the loss he felt when his relationship with his son was threatened.

The day the child welfare agency knocked on Deron's door, his world fell apart. An allegation had surfaced, with an anonymous party claiming that Deron had inappropriately touched his son. Deron had never committed a crime, much less harmed his own son. With Roy removed from his care, Deron quickly became a stranger to the very love that had once lit up his life. On top of that, Deron now wore the label of a menace, a perceived threat to society, all while his heart ached with the devastating realization that he could not protect his boy.

Faced with the legal entanglements that followed, Deron's life became a daily battle, an ankle monitor strapped to his leg, a probation officer shadowing his every move. He felt like a ghost in his own existence. He mourned and grieved the loss of his old life. Deron eventually found himself in my office, his spirit badly beaten. Each week, we sat together, peeling back the layers of fear and despair, exploring his inner child that had once been so vibrant and full of hope.

Deron's attorney suggested a plea deal, which would require admitting guilt to a crime he never committed. It was a one-way ticket to further despair, and yet, a part of Deron believed it might be his only escape from the agony. He came to me one session, his voice shaking.

"I'm going to take the plea," he said. At that moment, I was reminded of my mother's powerful words, instilling resilience in times of strife. I thought of her gentle encouragement that always reminded me, "You are somebody."

With renewed determination, I leaned in and met his gaze. "You are innocent, Deron. You won't take this plea." I watched as his slumped posture straightened, a spark igniting in his weary eyes. This was not just a fight for himself but for the love of his son.

"What time is it?" I asked, breaking the heavy silence. With a small smile creeping back onto his face, he said the mantra that I instilled into the guys I worked with.

"GAME TIME!"

In that moment, I could tell Deron was not ready to throw in the towel. Together, we searched for another attorney, one who believed in Deron's innocence and was willing to confront the accusing voices.

In the weeks that followed, Deron was no longer alone in his fight to clear his name and get his son back. A village of fathers surrounded him, creating a support system woven from love, understanding, and shared experiences. They brought with them encouragement, heartfelt hugs, and additional strength to counter the darkness that sought to consume him.

Finally, the storm began to break. As evidence emerged and whispers of truth surfaced, the charges against Deron crumbled. The family that had made the allegations admitted it was a lie, a terrible misunderstanding that had spiraled out of control.

When the call came that Roy would be returned, tears of joy streamed down Deron's face. The weight of shame and sadness lifted, replaced by the overwhelming love for the boy he had fought so hard to get back. As Roy ran into his dad's arms, their bond was forged stronger through adversity. Deron finally felt whole again.

In a world that had threatened to label him forever, Deron

emerged not just as a father, but as a fighter, proving that love, resilience, and unity could shatter the most insidious of lies. Deron knew now, not only was he somebody, but he was everything to his son, and together they would reclaim the narrative of their lives, one day at a time. The fear and grief of loss, while consuming Deron temporarily, did not prevail.

If we don't confront loss and grief, the results can be deadly. I know this firsthand.

In the summer of 2008, my emotions were so dark that I felt completely isolated and powerless. I was attending a summer institute in North Carolina, staying in a dorm room. I can't remember why, but those intense feelings of worthlessness and inadequacy took over that summer. I couldn't imagine a future. This is a dangerous place to be for a young man.

During one particularly challenging period, I looked up from my bed and noticed that the dorm window was open. I walked over to it. I stared at the open window, imagining myself putting one foot up on the sill, then the other. It would all be over so quickly. The pain would be over. The suffering would end. The loss and grief was too much.

Mercifully, my suicidal ideation remained just that: a terrible, dark idea that momentarily seized control of my thoughts. But I will never forget the images that plagued my mind in those few minutes. The thought of my foot on the window rail overlooking the college campus remains imprinted in my mind when I think about the power of pain. What was it that even made me consider ending my life?

I've reflected on that moment many times, and I remember that while standing at the window, I was unable to find any meaning or worth. Thankfully, I could still see that deep down, there was something left for me to achieve on this earth. That belief saved my life. If it had not been for that inner belief, that my higher power had something more extraordinary in store for me, I would have jumped out of that window. Even today, it takes courage and strength to live with these memories still imprinted on my psyche.

There's not really a silver lining to these kinds of traumatic events. But in retrospect, this moment was integral to developing a system of ethics that would lead me to become a servant to fathers needing guidance and love.

After watching fathers attend school functions with my peers, displaying genuine interest in the well-being of my classmates, I believed from the beginning that everyone needed a father who was present in their lives. This belief led me to think that I was somehow damaged or unlovable because I didn't have a father around. I cycled through grief—denial, anger, bargaining, depression, and acceptance. I tried to bargain with my mother, asking her to let me go live with my father. But I came to accept the fact that my father, at least for now, would not be physically and emotionally involved in my life, nor would he fit the image of my friends' fathers. I "accepted" this reality. At least that's what I told myself.

Anger has played an outsize role in my life. I had been angry for years because of my father's absence. My rage had harmed others, including my mother, who dealt with the projection of my anger on countless occasions. When I was younger, I took out most of the anger on her even when she tried her best.

I've also struggled with anxiety, which interfered with my ability to perform as an athlete and student. This anxiety resulted in a subsequent body image condition that caused me to stare in the mirror, exercise excessively, and hurt areas of my body that I labeled ugly. My emotions were dominated by stress, anger, and feelings of worthlessness. Anxiety was everywhere. My life seemed destined for choppiness.

At one point in this journey, I focused heavily on bargaining. My mother had one requirement in her household, and that was to attend church service consistently. This rule allowed her to ensure that I was surrounded by a community of individuals who cared about me and who believed in a power higher than themselves. But my grief about my father turned even this pleasant part of my life into a negative. I relied on prayer, Scripture, and the notion that God would reward those who remained faithful to Him. The reward I hoped for was that my father would return to be a part of my life, which I desperately wanted. Even when I was made aware of why he had not been actively engaged in my life, that he had another family, I still believed there was hope. I recognize now that this hope was probably not healthy, that I was engaged in a typical form of bargaining, with God or with the universe. Back then, though, I prayed that if I lived a good enough life, I would be rewarded with my father's return.

Accepting the reality that I would not have the privilege of being raised by an engaged father was difficult. For a child who wants desperately to know and be loved by his dad, it's all but impossible.

Even though I suffered from the loss of a father, I gained an understanding of the phenomenon of father-absenteeism that I would not have felt so viscerally if it had not been for this loss. I learned that my experience with my dad's unresolved struggles, bereavement, and grief, and the symptoms I experienced because of that, could be better used to contribute to the world. I decided to focus my life's work on understanding father-absenteeism and fatherlessness.

What I've learned from processing my experience with my

father is that every person has a purpose that is far greater than themselves, that understanding that purpose is often painful and difficult, that allowing our purpose to fill the void will renew how we interact with the world, and that we can use our purpose to help others find theirs.

Understanding that our purpose in life should lead to serving others is a power greater than oneself. Acts of service result in a personal transformation. A sense of purpose has given me the strength to walk upright, despite trials and tribulations. And it has given me a mission.

Lesson: Force yourself to find the purpose. A student's purpose is as precious as gold. We should never assume that a student does not have one. Even if it's not immediately apparent, we must strive to uncover it because the effort will be rewarding in the end.

One of our goals at Fathers' UpLift is teaching men the importance of presence, usually in the context of being with their children. But there's another aspect to presence that is equally important, even if it's not always easy to remember. The mistaken idea that our current circumstances are permanent can be crippling. I try to remind the men I'm coaching that they are not defined by their pasts, and also that they can shape their future. Nothing is predetermined. But even I sometimes have difficulty remembering the art of being present. Which is why I often come back to the story of George.

George Akwasi-Oduro Boakye-Yiadom Sr. was born in Ghana, and while he relocated to Pittsburgh when he was a child, he maintains a strong love for and appreciation of his African roots and identity. George is warm, funny, and a talented communicator. He's a great dad to his three kids and a devoted husband to his wife, Ivy.

But when I met George back in 2016, his life was filled with challenges.

A case worker, George fell ill at work one day, collapsing to the floor. He was only in his thirties, so the fact that he lost all his strength and was having trouble breathing was particularly troubling. He was diagnosed with cardiomyopathy. His heart could not pump blood efficiently, and within a few months he had endured a series of setbacks, including several strokes.

"I'm dying," he told Ivy.

George required open-heart surgery, which meant long stays in the hospital. With most of his family back in Ghana, George didn't have the support network needed for such an arduous recovery. I visited when I could, but with one small kid at home, and Samantha and me trying to get our nonprofit off the ground, I couldn't be there for George as much as I would have liked.

Ivy was living in Atlanta and did what she could to help. She eventually decided to enroll in graduate school up in Boston so that she could be closer. Their bond was tight, and Ivy was committed to doing what she could to make the recovery process easier. She accompanied George to appointments, learned to change his dressings, and deciphered the various beeps from the machines keeping him alive.

For all his charm and determination, George could be stubborn, prideful, and egotistical at times. Ivy knew he needed help, both to confront the emotional turmoil that accompanies illness, and to deal with the challenges of being estranged from his child back in Pennsylvania.

Ivy got to work, scanning the profiles of therapists and counselors in *Psychology Today*.

"And there you were, smiling ear to ear," Ivy recalled when we talked about how she found me as a resource for George.

Though addressing mental health still faces some stigma in the African American community, Ivy persuaded George to meet up with me. Our office in Roxbury, a neighborhood of Boston, was not exactly spacious. A man my height can pretty easily touch both walls with arms outstretched.

George didn't want to be there. He told me that the only reason he agreed to meet was because he felt he had hit rock bottom. What did he have to lose?

That kind of attitude isn't uncommon among some of the folks I've counseled over the years, but it isn't ideal, either. When I think back to Dr. Owens, my mentor in college, I remember him saying that the reason we worked well together was partly because I was "coachable." Or put another way, I was willing to give his advice a shot. If that attitude isn't present when a man comes to me for counsel, it might not work.

But despite his reservations, George seemed open to seeing how I could help him.

"I thought therapy was another scam, just somebody trying to make money," George told me recently. "I could talk to my friends." Plus, in Ghanaian culture, George said, therapy was suspect. People relied on prayer and their pastors to get through difficult times. But Ivy saw that George was suffering and asked him several times if he would consider trying out therapy. She had sacrificed so much for him, so he decided to give it a go. Even if he wasn't fully on board, if meeting me made Ivy happy, he'd go ahead with it.

I was curious what made George lower his guard a bit and trust me during those earliest meetings. He told me that first of all, just seeing me helped. While I'm used to being one of the tallest guys in any room, George is more than six and a half feet tall. Like George, I'm also Black. So that first meeting,

George saw someone who looked like him. He said that when he pictured "therapy," he imagined an older white guy sitting in a chair, taking notes and judging him.

"Going to see a middle-aged white guy, that wouldn't have worked," George told me. "He wouldn't have resonated with me."

When he saw me, those fears were put to rest. People want to feel like the therapist they are opening up to understands where they are coming from, which is why there need to be more opportunities for Black and Hispanic men to become therapists. I'm not sure if George would have been open to receiving the help he needed had he been unable to find someone who he trusted could understand him.

George also told me that our meetings "didn't feel like therapy." Rather, he said that he felt like a friend was listening to him, that he had found someone who believed in him and who cared about his life. He liked that I didn't talk down to him or make him feel like he was a medical specimen. "You didn't make me feel dumb," he told me. Instead, we talked about his challenges in simple ways.

And one of those challenges was his relationship with his daughter.

At that point, George hadn't seen his daughter with any regularity for four years. At first, there were disagreements with his daughter's mother. Then the trek from Boston to Pittsburgh grew to feel even longer with each visit. And with the onset of George's heart issues, spending all that time in the hospital recovering made visits virtually impossible. With George's presence in their daughter's life uneven at best, her mother decided it just wasn't worth it. She cut off all contact.

But George didn't see it that way, at least not at first. He was angry, first at his daughter's mother for keeping her away from him, and next at himself for not being the kind of dad he knew he could be. I listened to his concerns and tried to help him see things from the point of view of his daughter and her mother.

"In the beginning, I was angry, because I felt ready to be a father and wanted my child there," George recalled. "But you helped me remember that it doesn't work that way. Just because I'm ready doesn't mean the mother is."

When George decided he was ready to be more present in his daughter's life, I coached him on the best ways to broach the idea with her mother. George met with me for one-on-one counseling. He attended group sessions, where he met other men facing similar parenting challenges. I wanted to create a space where Black men could feel safe to talk candidly about their emotions. George joked with me later that when he started attending the group sessions, he could understand just two emotions: happiness and anger. But by talking about his experiences with other men, he learned a lot more.

During those groups, I talked with the men about emotional combat and the need for us to manage our emotions so that they don't control us.

George flew to Pittsburgh to visit for his daughter's birthday. He made plans to go again, and slowly but surely, they rebuilt their relationship.

Over time, and with lots of effort, George created a closer bond with his daughter. He visits as often as he can and even has plans to bring her on a visit to Ghana along with Ivy and their two kids.

George overcame a lot in order to become the kind of dad

he believed he could be, and his grit and determination made me realize he could help others. So when Samantha and I decided we needed help with some of our programming at Fathers' UpLift, we asked George. At first, he was hesitant. We had wanted him to lead a group for kids, and he said he had no idea how he could possibly help. But part of my method is instilling confidence in the men I work with. I told George he'd be great and asked him to trust me.

George is a walking inspiration. I told him that running a youth group was nothing compared to the obstacles he had overcome.

"I don't know how you're gonna do it, but I know you'll figure it out," I told him. "I have faith in you."

Sure enough, he helped grow the program, and the kids loved him.

George told me later that being part of Fathers' UpLift as a staff member gave him a huge boost of confidence. For much of his life, people had been telling George that he was never enough: not smart enough, not good enough, not around enough. But here I was, he said, telling him that he was exactly what we needed. He had felt hampered by the medical challenges he faced, and as a result, he risked losing his very identity. Ivy said that for years, it seemed like George had lost his purpose in life and couldn't figure out why he was still here. After his coaching and involvement with Fathers' UpLift, she said, George found that inner drive.

"In the beginning, he had lost a reason to live, and that's a dangerous place to be," Ivy recounted. "I'm so thankful because he found that his life was still worth fighting for."

When I think of George's example of being present, I am transported to a moment we shared a few days before he received his heart transplant. Though it happened many years ago now, the memory of this encounter is still difficult for me to recount, but it's necessary for the purpose of my efforts to understand the power of presence.

George had been hospitalized for some time, becoming weaker as he awaited a desperately needed transplant. Several of my team members had made the journey to Tufts Medical Center in downtown Boston to visit, and they kept everyone updated on George's condition.

I was talking to Samantha one night about George.

"Do you think he's going to make it through this?" she asked me.

I assumed that she was looking for reassurance that our friend would be okay. But given everything I was hearing about George's struggle, I wasn't so sure myself.

"I asked God, but I didn't hear an answer back," I said.

It was one of the few times during the whole ordeal that I felt lost, without an answer, unable to offer confident certainty. Samantha felt that and appeared devastated by my answer.

The updates kept coming, and things seemed to be getting worse for George. Whenever I pictured him lying in his hospital bed, attached to various machines and unable to breathe on his own, my heart sank. I vowed to visit him, so that I could at least offer some emotional support during what I knew was a trying time for him. But each time I planned a visit, I found an excuse not to go. Work. Kids. Deadlines. The truth was, even though I prayed ceaselessly for George to have the strength to hold on until a new heart arrived, I just couldn't bring myself to see my friend in that state. I was in pain and felt helpless. And each time I failed to show up, I felt ashamed. It was a vicious cycle.

But with encouragement from Samantha, and after some

self-coaching, I mustered up the courage and got myself to Tufts one day after work.

Wet from the rain, I entered the hospital and found George's room. I took a deep breath and steeled myself for the pain I'd feel in seeing my friend like this. I wondered if he would be upset that I hadn't been by sooner or if he'd even be able to talk at all. I had convinced myself that all the worst-case scenarios would play out, and I began to worry. But when I entered George's room, I was surprised by what I encountered.

There was George, situated in a hospital bed like I had imagined. He had lost an excessive amount of weight and could barely speak with all the tubes going through his body. His mother stood on the opposite side of the bed, her eyes welled up. Despite all that, George seemed to emanate a state of calm.

As I offered a forced smile to hide my sadness, the three of us sat silently, until the nurse made her round to check on George and inspect the bandages wrapped around his body. I was overcome with sadness and felt like tears were imminent. But I did not want George to see me cry, not at that moment, anyway. I felt like I had to stay strong for him. After all, he was the one going through this, not me. George periodically stared at me, and then away, in silence.

"Charles, can you pray for me?"

I looked up in shock, barely able to hold myself together.

"Yes, let's pray . . ." I said.

George, his mother, and I proceeded to pray. I didn't articulate it, of course, but I doubted God at that moment. But it was clear to me that George didn't, and who was I to voice any objection to his sincere request. He knew where his final word would come from.

"Lord, George will make it through this," I prayed. "Allow Your will to be done, and knowing Your will, he will live another day with the ability to be present for his children and loved ones as they grow older. We stand in agreement, knowing that this will be the case. In Your Son's name we pray. Amen."

It occurs to me now that in some ways, the prayer was selfish. I wanted God to keep George here for us, even more than for himself. But I didn't care. It was my prayer.

Looking back, I can see more clearly the battle that George was up against, which was the fight to be present in the moment beyond the dire circumstances he faced. George, even in his hospital bed, lived unscathed by the mere fact that his heart was failing. His body may have been in a state of sickness, but his spirit was present enough to request that we gather in the presence of his God. The contrast between his bodily state and his ability to be present at that moment with his mother and me remains one of the most courageous things I have ever witnessed. I saw, in just a few seconds, the power of his mind and the weakness of his body. If he had lost his spirit, he would not be here today.

In the years since that encounter, George and I have talked about his ethos of living, which is to be present in all things, so that he can lead a life where joy stands firmly in even the most challenging situations. During his long recovery, George created a clothing line, traveled the world, regained access to his daughter, and continued to give back—all while fighting for his life. Depression, fear, and even the ventricular-assist device that threatened to derail George didn't stop him from being a father to his children and a husband to Ivy.

I recently asked him what he was thinking in his hospital bed the day I visited him.

"George, man, that was close . . ." I said, still unable to voice the reality that we had nearly lost him.

His response was simple.

"My family needed me," he said. "Even while on that bed, hope was present with me—it never left."

The hope to live and be present another day is ingrained in the fabric of George's being. He chooses to live boldly, undeterred by the nature of his circumstances. George's approach to being present is to live moment by moment. Tribulations are beauty marks, not deficits. During all that he was undergoing, George held firmly to the privilege of creating memories with those he loved rather than fixating on the things he could not control.

When I think my life is horrible or even question my work, I remind myself to "Live Like George." By that, I mean remaining aware of the beauty of the opportunity to be present each day. When you are preoccupied with the beauty of life, more so than the challenges, you'll remain present. The preoccupation, for some, is a choice. George chose life a while ago, a few days after learning of his illness. Half the battle was won the day he decided that he would live like he had never received a prognosis that, in reality, had permanently altered his life.

None of this is to say that sheer willpower or positive thinking can inoculate anyone against the many challenges life throws our way. I have also known people whose spirits seemed inextinguishable, who vowed to fight no matter what came their way, but who ultimately lost their battles with various illnesses. Sometimes, even the most determined person is no match for medical realities.

But with George, although his prognosis was ever present, he didn't let it define him. We have a choice not to allow the prognoses of our lives to determine how we show up each second we're granted. To be present is to choose wisely—and it's not a one-time decision. Choosing to be present is a state of being, one that must be nourished and nurtured every moment of every day.

Lesson: Hope is ever present even when unseen. Hope exists even when it's not visible. It's a constant presence, offering reassurance and optimism, even when we can't perceive it. Often, the student must know that we see it.

---

15. BAGS FOR DADS

I n our work, Samantha and I regularly encounter signs that the so-called system is broken. It would be easy to throw up our hands and walk away, but that's not helpful for anyone. Still, sometimes even well-meaning people become inured to the systemic challenges facing society. Whether it's the need to expand access to health care, protecting the environment, or helping men become good dads, the task can feel overwhelming, and lots of people simply give up. It's true that systemic injustices are not easily fixed and often require buy-in from political, civic, and business leaders. But that doesn't mean that everyday folks can't make a big change in the lives of vulnerable people. Take Bags for Dads, a program Samantha started after she observed a routine injustice men leaving prison faced.

Early on in our work with Fathers' UpLift, Samantha noticed something that, in retrospect, seems so obvious, but at the time was a blind spot. This is one of Samantha's best characteristics, finding a need others overlook and then creating solutions.

Many of the men we work with are referred to Fathers' Up-

Lift by social workers after leaving prison. We had developed a reputation of being an effective partner for men trying to find their footing following incarceration, and for the guys who found their way to us, we stopped at nothing to make sure they had the support they needed during what could be a difficult transition.

Each year in the United States, more than 600,000 people are released from federal and state prisons, according to a 2024 report from the U.S. government.[26] Keeping those individuals out of jail requires not just the determination of the formerly incarcerated person, but a system committed to helping them achieve their goals. For Black men in particular, who are incarcerated in state prisons at rates as high as five times more than white men,[27] the challenge of staying out of jail is complicated by systemic injustices. This reality is discouraging.

The Justice Department released a report in 2018 that followed prisoners from twenty-four states for ten years after they were released. An astonishing 82 percent of the former prisoners were arrested again.[28] A separate report, from Brookings, noted that formerly incarcerated individuals face particularly challenging obstacles around employment, housing, establishing social networks, and developing skills.[29] One thing from all this research is clear: No formerly incarcerated man can make the transition work on his own. To do so requires support networks and strong partnerships.

But the key to those successful partnerships is making sure that the guys can gain access to resources. Otherwise, what good are resources if they aren't making their way to the people who need them in order to thrive? At Fathers' UpLift, we wanted to be partners, but we had to find a way to make sure we could develop relationships as early as possible. If we didn't, all the planning in the world wouldn't do much good.

"You all have so many dads behind bars who need your services," Samantha remembers being asked several times. "Why aren't you there? Shouldn't you offer programming behind bars, too?"

That made sense to Samantha, and she considered ways that Fathers' UpLift might help men prepare for life outside prison well before their release date. Her foresight paid off when one day a supporter of our work, Karla Walker, told us she was starting a consortium of support services at the correctional facility where she worked full-time. When Samantha heard this, she didn't hesitate in offering to work together.

"We've been trying to determine how we could work in the jails, but didn't know how to start," Samantha told Karla. Impressed by Samantha's determination to help address an unmet need, Karla arranged for Fathers' UpLift to be able to offer programming inside the prison.

But *what* programming?

One thing that's always impressed me about Samantha is the way she can apply academic theory to concrete realities. She knew that we would be more effective partners with these men if we consulted with them about their needs before telling them what we could do for them. For therapists and case workers assisting people of color, especially men, it's essential to establish a strong relationship based on mutual trust. Otherwise, many of these men, who have previously been let down by the system, won't take us at our word when we tell them that we can help. That meant we needed to develop relationships before a man was released from jail. Samantha was working full-time at another agency, helping parents learn the skills they needed to be good moms and dads. I saw clients all day, and Samantha would leave work, pick up Clayton from daycare, and head to Fathers' UpLift to help with administrative tasks. On weekends, she saw clients, too. After two years of this, we were both running ourselves ragged. When a colleague put a bug in Samantha's ear that she should consider working full-time at Fathers' UpLift, Samantha was intrigued but also a bit nervous. To do so would require a big leap of faith, not in our mission, which she fully supported, but in our capacity to grow and expand. But it was a risk she was willing to take.

It paid off. We developed a program for incarcerated men to help with their transition to life outside jail, and signed a ten-year partnership agreement with the local jail. This would allow us to make a long-term commitment to this work and ensure that we could keep growing our organization. At this point Samantha decided it made sense to devote her time fully to Fathers' UpLift, and she got to work.

We heard over and over how difficult the transition could be from prison to the outside world, especially if the men had been incarcerated for a long time. Society changes so fast, relationships fray, and children grow up. Trying to reconnect with wives or girlfriends could be difficult enough. Throw children into the mix, and it could get messy fast. Samantha and I had worked with enough men coming out of prison to know how each man's story is unique and requires a comprehensive plan to address various challenges. But what about day one? That's what we kept hearing in our conversations with men still inside the prison.

A comment from one father in particular, Jeff, stuck with us. Samantha had been working with Jeff for about three months, helping him to prepare for life "outside the walls," as she put it. Building trust is the most important thing a case worker can do, and Samantha and Jeff had hit it off. As Jeff was getting ready to be released, what should have been a moment of relief for him instead racked him with anxiety.

"No one is gonna be here to pick me up," Jeff told Samantha. He would leave the Suffolk County House of Corrections with a bus pass in hand. Taking the bus wasn't the issue. Instead, it was the walk he'd have to make from the jail to the bus stop. Jeff would have to pass through the infamous Methadone Mile, a stretch of the city that *The Boston Globe* described as "the congested heart of Massachusetts' raging opioid crisis."[30] The area is home to a number of social services providers, a hospital, and lots of people looking to find drugs to feed their addictions. Most people could keep their heads down and power walk through the area, but Jeff wasn't most people. He was in recovery and determined to turn around his life. But he knew that he wasn't in a place to walk through Methadone Mile unscathed.

"By the time I get to the bus, I am going to be high," Jeff told Samantha.

In his admission we heard shame, guilt, fear, anxiety, and hurt. It wasn't a threat, but an acknowledgment that once he was on his own, Jeff would turn to what he knew, and with no outside support to make sure he got the help he needed, he'd fall back into harmful patterns.

Samantha had an idea. Perhaps instead of walking out of the prison by himself, a bus ticket in hand and nothing but anxiety on the horizon, Jeff could instead be met by somebody who wanted him to succeed, somebody who could help.

"I'll pick you up!" Samantha offered.

Jeff looked at her with skepticism. He wasn't used to people lending him a helping hand. Plus, it wasn't as simple as getting a ride from the jail to the halfway house where he'd be staying.

"I need to cash a check, then check in with my parole officer," Jeff said.

"Okay, I'll meet you and we'll get it all done," Samantha told him.

The day of Jeff's release, Samantha arrived at the jail and waited for him. When he spotted her, Jeff looked amazed. Someone had actually shown up for him.

"I told you I was gonna be here!" Samantha said with a smile.

Once he was ready to go, Jeff was handed a clear plastic garbage bag containing all his belongings. He tied it up and slung it over his shoulder, ready to get on with his life. But something about that bag caught Samantha's eye. She pushed her thoughts aside and called a rideshare.

The car pulled up and Samantha noticed how the driver eyed Jeff's bag as he put it into the trunk for the drive to the check-cashing store. Once they arrived, Samantha asked if the driver could wait a few minutes while Jeff cashed his check so they could make their way to the parole officer.

"Sorry, but I can't," he said. "Gotta go."

Samantha waited while Jeff got out of the car and retrieved the garbage bag from the trunk. They headed into the check-cashing store together. Jeff carried the bag over his shoulder, and Samantha felt everyone's eyes prying into him as he entered. Jeff had obviously just gotten out of jail, and though he didn't articulate it at that moment, Samantha knew that he felt shame, embarrassment, and guilt. All those missed birthdays and holidays. His mistakes now colored what others thought of him. It was as if Jeff's whole identity was reduced to this single plastic bag. It struck Samantha as wrong, that a moment that was supposed to signify a fresh start somehow seemed to tie Jeff even more securely to his past.

Samantha, ever upbeat and effervescent, tried to recalibrate what could have been just one more traumatizing situation for

Jeff. She offered an encouraging word, helped him cash the check, and called another car. She waited with Jeff and accompanied him to an appointment with his probation officer. Then, they stopped for lunch. Samantha wanted to show Jeff that he could rely on her, and Fathers' UpLift, to help him through these stressful moments.

On her way back to our office, Samantha couldn't shake the image of Jeff standing there with his plastic bag. It seemed unnecessarily cruel, a sort of modern-day scarlet letter that let everyone know Jeff had done time. By the time she arrived, Samantha had an idea, simultaneously simple and brilliant. Through our work with men who were still incarcerated, we would be able to develop relationships before a man was released from prison, so that when he was released, a familiar face was there waiting for him. A degree of trust would be developed, and he'd stand a chance at success during those first, crucial hours.

A few days later, Samantha checked in with Jeff to see how he was faring at the halfway house. He was getting on, but he couldn't find money to buy fresh T-shirts, underwear, and towels.

"I can help with that," Samantha offered. She helped Jeff get some basics, hoping that it meant he would stick it out at the halfway house and not fall back into harmful patterns. Whatever she could do to make Jeff feel like he was making progress, she did.

That's how Samantha came up with the idea of Bags for Dads, a program we created at Fathers' UpLift to ensure that men who are leaving prison would not be subject to the judgmental stares of strangers who saw their possessions shoved into a garbage bag.

Going forward, each time someone from Fathers' UpLift

met a man being released from prison, they'd present a sturdy black duffel bag, filled with an assortment of items many of us take for granted: a comb, a toothbrush and toothpaste, shampoo, deodorant, and a resource card listing the phone numbers of people and places who could help with the transition. On the front is the Fathers' UpLift logo and our phone number.

More than the bag or its contents, though, this tool brings with it a sense of dignity. It helps these men blend in as they go about trying to put their lives back together. The bag is a sign that someone cares. Samantha's goal was to ensure that no dad experienced the same "walk of shame" that accompanied Jeff as he reentered society—and she succeeded.

Each bag costs Fathers' UpLift about $80, and we are fortunate to partner with community organizations who collect hygiene items to donate and sometimes host fundraisers. We work with schools for "bag packing" days, and we take satisfaction in seeing how our concept has been adopted by other organizations and agencies.

In the years since Samantha came up with the idea of Bags for Dads, Fathers' UpLift has expanded the program to ensure that men have a full range of support as they transition from life "behind the walls" back to life with their families and children. We pack hundreds of bags a year as part of working with men inside prison and standing by them once they get out. The bags are simple, but they're also a powerful reminder that somebody cares, that nobody should be expected to walk this journey alone.

The impact of Bags for Dads extends beyond just providing physical items. It's a testament to the power of empathy and understanding in our society. By offering support to these men, we show them that they are not alone and we advocate for changes to public life. This program urges us to recognize the value of second chances, the importance of rehabilitation, and the need to foster a supportive community for individuals seeking to reintegrate into society after incarceration.

Through the Bags for Dads initiative, we encourage others to consider what they can do to support those incarcerated, understand the challenges they face, and advocate for systemic changes that promote successful reentry into the community. It's a reminder that everyone has a role in creating a more inclusive and compassionate society. Sometimes solutions to society's challenges are complex, require action from powerful institutions, and can take months or years to implement. Sometimes, however, it simply takes a kind heart and some ingenuity.

> **Lesson:** Don't underestimate the simple things we take for granted. Dignity and self-respect lie beneath the simple things.

16. TRAINING FUTURE PRACTITIONERS

I n the United States, it's difficult for nearly everyone to access mental health care. But for Black Americans, it can feel almost impossible. That's why people like Tim C. Levers are so important.

I met Tim more than a decade ago, when he approached me seeking an internship at Fathers' UpLift. We were a young organization, short on resources and definitely unable to wow potential interns with perks that might have been available at bigger practices. Those early days at Fathers' UpLift, when Tim wanted to join the team, weren't easy. I was lucky to have received a generous but ultimately pretty small grant to help us get started, and I gave myself a salary of just $10,000 a year. With a son at home, and Samantha still in school, times were tight. I regularly faced a decision of whether to spend the small amount of money in my bank account on bills or formula.

But Tim, who called himself a "late bloomer" because he was studying for his master's in social work in his forties, had the kind of infectious energy that I was confident would benefit the guys who sought help at Fathers' UpLift. And there were a lot of people to help.

Barriers to care are well documented and affect every population, but Black Americans face a unique set of challenges. According to a 2022 report from the American Psychological Association, just 5 percent of the psychological workforce in the United States is Black, compared to 12 percent of the general population. That same report shows that finding a Black male counselor is even tougher.[31] And perhaps because of this, in addition to the historic mistrust of a medical system that has mistreated them, Black Americans are less likely than white Americans to seek mental health care overall.

When Tim arrived for his interview, I made sure to stop by to introduce myself and try to sell him on Fathers' UpLift. I knew he was looking at a couple of other options, but I hoped that he'd see our mission as important. And I promised him that he would get the kind of hands-on experience with us that might not be available at bigger organizations. He left. I waited. And sure enough, he accepted our offer.

It's not easy to understand without experiencing it firsthand, but there's a rush of positive energy and goodwill that permeates the atmosphere at Fathers' UpLift. Part of that comes from me. I pump up the team, reminding them that this is a group effort and that it takes lots of energy to make it over the finish line. Come into any office or group session where I'm present, and you'll almost certainly hear a loud "Game time! Let's go!" chant coming from me. Tim picked up on that and wanted to be in on the action.

On the second day of Tim's internship, he approached me and told me about his plans to become a therapist. I couldn't have been happier for him. I knew that his personal story and his very being made him an ideal fit for the great need I saw in our community and around the country.

"Good, I'm glad to hear that," I told him. "And there's a client waiting for you in the other room."

Tim stammered.

"But I still have some work to do before I can see clients," he said.

He was right, in the technical sense. No matter.

"No, you're a therapist today," I shot back, eager to offer encouragement.

Tim reminded me of this story years later. He said that those words, "You're a therapist today," stuck with him through the years. He said he trusted me enough that, even though he felt like I was tossing him into the deep end before he knew how to swim, I'd never let him sink. When Tim returned from the session, I asked him how it went. He said the client seemed pleased, but that he still hadn't finished reading up on the various tools one needs in order to be an effective therapist.

"It doesn't matter how much book knowledge you have," I told him. "You can read all the theory you want, but when you go into that room, you're interviewing. They are the specialists of their own lives. You have to be willing to connect with people."

I knew Tim had what it took to connect with the clients we served, so I harbored no reservations about him jumping into the deep end.

Tim grew up in Dorchester, the same neighborhood where our office was located. He actually remembered hanging out in front of the building when he was a kid. It used to be a radio station, and he and his friends would hope to catch glimpses of on-air talent when they left work. Years later, Tim said the neighborhood wasn't as safe as he'd like, but it was still home.

And what drew him to Fathers' UpLift was that we were a resource for the local community.

"Random brothers would walk in off the street, sit down, have coffee, and just talk," he recalled of those early days. "This place felt like I could be myself here."

Tim worked in human services for a number of years and noticed how his friends and acquaintances regularly approached him for advice. He liked hearing their stories and doled out advice he if thought he could help. That insight led him to seek a career in therapy, even if it took a bit longer to get there than he planned. He told me that his role model for this kind of service was his dad, who raised him with the help of an aunt who lived above them in the same building. His dad both fathered and mothered him, he said, waking him up for school, making him breakfast, and ensuring he finished his homework. If Tim acted up, his father got him back in line. Tim's dad was a hard worker, going in for night shifts as a supervisor at Gillette to make sure there was enough money to take care of the family's needs while Tim's aunt checked in from upstairs.

In addition to inspiring others to seek careers in counseling, Tim's story can help to reframe how society sees fathers more broadly.

He chose his career path partly because of his own father, who sacrificed to give Tim a good life, employing a kind of parenting that even fathers who co-parent with their children's mothers could incorporate into their own lives so that they can develop an even closer relationship with their kids.

While Tim was lucky to have a close relationship with his loving father, some of his friends and family didn't have that same luck. He saw too much fatherlessness in his community, and he wanted to help. Tim never forgot how much his father sacrificed for his family, and when he saw the kind of work we do at Fathers' UpLift, he was on board instantly.

I watched Tim grow into the kind of therapist I would send my closest friends and family to without hesitation.

One-on-one, Tim is an excellent counselor, in part because his sincere curiosity about the lives of other people and his empathy for their struggles seem to compel his every move. I remember how he patiently counseled one man who had just finished a long stretch of incarceration, during which he had lost contact with his kids.

This father came to us because he wanted to mend those relationships, but he didn't know where to begin. He had gone more than a decade without seeing his children, which was partly his decision. He didn't want his kids to see him in jail—his shame clouded his vision—so he decided he'd rather not see them at all. Plus, his struggles with addiction and homelessness meant he didn't have the stability he felt he needed to be a good dad. Quite frankly, this man held on to a lot of baggage he needed to overcome before a healthy reunion would be possible. Perhaps understandably, the mother of his children was apprehensive about him wanting to reestablish contact after so many years away. Plus, the logistics would be challenging. Men leaving jail and prison are often rebuilding their lives from scratch, and they frequently lack the resources or networks that so many of us sometimes take for granted. Or put another way, if he didn't have a home where he felt comfortable hosting such a reunion, what was he to do?

Tim encouraged the man to be honest about his feelings. He could sense the fear, fragility, and shame that seemed to possess him during every conversation about a possible reunion. Tim worked with this man for more than two years, and with Tim's encouragement, he invited his kids to meet him at Fathers' UpLift, a neutral place for the reunion. Tim wasn't aware of the financial challenges we as an organization were facing back then, but he was impressed that we offered the space to this man, and to many like him, free of charge. Other organizations might charge a fee, but I saw it as our duty to do everything we could to reunite kids with their dads. Men in this position are sometimes faced with the agonizing dilemma of whether they should spend the few bucks they have left on food for themselves or for a safe space to see their kids.

The meeting took place, and Tim debriefed with the man afterward, asking what he felt during the reunion. Tim answered his questions and helped him imagine a future. He eventually found a place to live and still sees his children. Tim told me that he still sees this man around the neighborhood and that, while they aren't quite friends, they developed a fellowship of sorts. He still reaches out to Tim from time to time for advice, or even just to share some good news about his children. It took years of counseling for this man to be able to trust others in the community, to forgive himself for being away from his children, and to regain the confidence he needed to be a father again. Had Tim not chosen to use his gifts as a therapist, in his own community, who knows how this man's life would have ended up?

While Fathers' UpLift is an organization, with offices and therapy rooms and group meetings, it's also a movement. We aim to empower men whose lives haven't gone as they've wanted to equip themselves with the resources they need to be the kinds of fathers that they know deep down they can be. People like Tim help make this movement what it is.

Tim eventually ventured out on his own and established a practice in West Roxbury, another neighborhood of Boston with a sizable Black and Hispanic population. More than half his clients are couples, and he's particularly interested in helping Black families navigate the challenges life throws their way. He's still involved in Fathers' UpLift, as a faculty member of our United States Therapist Recruitment Fellowship, through which he's currently mentoring more than a dozen young people of color who want to enter the therapy field. He regularly visits high schools and colleges to encourage people with backgrounds like his own to consider therapy and counseling careers.

It was a privilege to see Tim, one of my first student interns, exhibit a characteristic I knew very well: His eyes were fixed firmly on what he wanted to do with his life once he graduated with his master's degree in social work. Tim didn't care about being unsure of how he would get there. He just knew the outcome would be what he envisioned. There's a saying that you must see where you want to be in this life before you get there. In Tim's case, this rings true. He exhibited it in every respect.

Tim's approach to being present consists of staying humble and finding a vision. He had no problem learning from those around him, regardless of age or socioeconomic status. I am younger than Tim, but he allowed me to impart knowledge, to show him what was possible in this sector. His ability to learn in a manner such as this originated from his observations of his father. In his example, learning goes both ways. He both teaches his children and receives knowledge from them. I feel lucky to have been part of his journey.

The second component of this example of being present is vision. Tim knows where he's going and has no problem with communicating this to others. Some people might be too embarrassed to talk about their dreams, perhaps afraid that they might not succeed. But Tim was never like this. The awareness of one's desired destination can be many things. For Tim, he knew that he was going to be unique. Knowing where you are situated and where you are going is integral to the ability to be present. When I told Tim that he would be a therapist that day we talked in my office, I knew deep down that he had everything he needed to become one. I knew this partially because of what he called himself. He said, unapologetically, after my coaching, "I am a therapist." He could see where he was headed, which motivated others, like me, to help him get there.

On the other hand, I also know that it's impossible to become anything that you are afraid to call yourself. If we can't speak life into our realities by recognizing that we are already what we intend to be, it becomes too overwhelming, convoluted, and even scary to work toward becoming that.

I referred to Tim as a therapist throughout his journey with me, which wasn't quite true at first; he still had exams to pass and clinical hours to complete. But I knew he was a therapist deep down, so it made sense to acknowledge that reality. Today, Tim is a therapist who's making a significant difference in the world. Being present has as much to do with the narratives we tell ourselves about who we are as it does with who the world tells us we are. We can't be present if our narratives are debilitating.

To be present is to be convinced that the moment is yours. How can you be something that you don't believe in? Tim's approach to being present aligns with the lessons we share with many of the men we serve, especially those fighting to be a part of their children's lives. The lesson is this: To be present means to know that you are already present as soon as you have decided to fight to be a part of your children's lives. You must see the image of yourself as the father you dreamed of being before your reality catches up. It might take years before a man is physically present with his children, especially when he has obstacles to overcome. But as soon as he decides he will do what it takes to make that dream a reality, he is present. And he must see himself as such. Perspective is crucial to being present.

Tim didn't relinquish my directive of entering that office and serving that man as the therapist he would one day become. While my request that he see our guest on his own was met initially with fear, Tim had already decided he was going to be a therapist. And that gave him the courage he needed to step up. He decided his fate that day.

Sometimes, the vision others have for you becomes a crutch until you find your voice. The power of words to shape realities is underappreciated today. Words are crucial when it comes to being present. They can propel you to soaring heights or keep you in a bind. What's essential is remembering that the words we articulate, or those spoken on our behalf, have the power to shape our realities.

There is nothing wrong with knowing what you want and where you are headed. When the opportunity to be present arises, your *why* and your *destination* will lead the way until your body catches up.

Lesson: Humility is learning. When learning no longer goes both ways, we've lost the student.

---

17. GRIT

Each morning, as my son Clayton gets ready for school, I ask him the same question. "What are you going to do today?"

By now, Clayton knows I'm not looking for an itinerary of his day or a list of the extracurriculars that will keep him busy after school. The answer is the same each and every day, and the whole exchange has become something of a warm-up routine for both of us as we begin our days.

"My best, Dad!" Clayton replies.

Clayton has repeated this answer hundreds of times by now, but it still makes my heart swell with pride each time I hear him say it. Because embedded in his answer is the implicit acknowledgement that in our home, we operate with a mindset that embraces both success and failure with equal enthusiasm. As a father, I try to instill in Clayton and SaMya the understanding that failure doesn't have to be a roadblock, but can instead be a stepping stone to growth. But I know that's easier said than done, which is why I'm intent on making sure Clayton and SaMya hear themselves say over and over and over again that doing their best is what's most important.

This isn't a lesson that came easy to me.

A couple of years ago, I decided to go public with something that had weighed heavily on me for a long time. In a series of essays I published on LinkedIn, I acknowledged the shame I felt after failing repeatedly to pass the exams required to become a licensed social worker.

I know what the data says about tests and how they affect people from marginalized communities. In my particular field, the Association of Social Work Boards publishes reports that show a stark contrast on the disparities among different racial groups. Black test takers have about a 40 percent chance of passing the exams, compared to 80 percent of white test takers. Addressing systemic barriers to equitable testing opportunities in order to broaden who has the chance to succeed in social work remains an important and ongoing project.

But knowing that information didn't make the sting of not succeeding on my first go feel any less painful. I know as a therapist that confronting our pasts directly and then talking through how certain events still impact us today is the healthiest way forward, but that doesn't mean it's pleasant. Nonetheless, I decided to confront my past failures directly, and called the organization that administers the exams. I wanted to know the exact dates of my failures so that I could put them in their proper context and begin to track my journey with the kind of clarity offered with hindsight.

At first, the person from the testing agency seemed a bit confused by my request. Instead of giving me the dates of my failed exams, he instead told me the dates when I finally passed the two exams. I can't say I blame him. Who wants to be reminded of when they failed a make-or-break exam?

I was eventually able to track down those dates. The first part of the exam was a written component—and I failed that on September 7, 2012, and again on January 3, 2013. Another four months went by before I finally passed. The clinical exam was even more brutal. My first attempt came on June 26, 2015, and nearly an entire year elapsed, along with three more tries, before I finally passed, on May 26, 2016. When I read the dates, I am jolted back in time, my chest tightens, and my face burns from embarrassment. But I also recall everything that went into those failures, including the lingering effects of poverty, my sometimes-crippling testing anxiety, the self-doubt that I have never fully vanquished, and the sadness I felt afterward, that my dreams might never come to fruition all because I couldn't pass a test.

It wasn't easy to talk publicly about the challenges I experienced in obtaining the licenses I needed to become an independent clinical social worker. I knew I ran the risk of people looking down on me, not just those who follow me on social media, but also the funders and partners I rely on to help my nonprofit grow. But I decided to do it anyway after I learned those dates and realized how important it is to be honest about our journeys.

The dates of my failed exams coincided with the hectic early days of Fathers' UpLift, when Samantha and I were devoting all our energy to getting it off the ground. In hindsight, it's no wonder I was having a difficult time with those exams. All my other challenges, combined with trying to nurture a fledgling nonprofit organization, plus our personal financial struggles, made the odds of passing incredibly unlikely. I couldn't see it clearly then, but looking back, it makes total sense.

This experience of looking back and learning from my mistakes and challenges informs my approach with the men I coach today. Persistence is key. It would have been reasonable for me to walk away from my dreams after failing my exam on my third try. Lots of people would have. But I stuck with it, because I knew that the mission of helping men become good dads was too important to give up on. By going public with my own story, I hoped to inspire others who have encountered obstacles along their journeys. It's unrealistic to think that any kind of success can be obtained without some bumps along the way. But we so seldom acknowledge these trials, which gives a warped perception of reality to people as they navigate uncharted territory.

We live in a society that conditions us to focus on success while glossing over challenges and setbacks that shape us. By embracing our failures, and by focusing on the growth that they nurture, we can change that narrative. Failure will always hurt, but it should be recognized as an essential step toward personal and professional growth.

On a personal level, my failure in passing the exams, along with other stumbles along the way, were pivotal in shaping me into the man I am today. They helped me develop resiliency, perseverance, and determination, while also providing opportunities to confront my limitations, learn to adapt to change, and trust that I will ultimately emerge stronger and more resilient. I have come to understand that failure is not the end, but rather a stepping stone to success.

There's also a bigger issue at play. Embracing and sharing our failures can pave the way for societal change. It can shatter the stigma surrounding failure and foster a culture of empathy, understanding, and support. When we openly acknowledge our failures, we create a space for others to do the same, fostering an environment where vulnerability is not a weakness but a source of strength.

I wasn't sure how I would feel publishing those essays online. After all, if there's a social media network that is not made for sharing failures, it's LinkedIn. But I decided to go ahead for a few reasons. First, there are a number of legislative efforts around the country aimed at making the test-taking process more equitable, and I want to lend my own voice to those efforts. Given the success I've achieved in the years since I failed those exams, I thought I could contribute to the debate by showing how Fathers' UpLift would never have materialized had I walked away from my career because of an unfair system.

Next, I seek to let others know that they aren't alone. The feedback I received from those essays showed me that there is a hunger for honesty when it comes not just to the disparities in our licensure processes, but also in how we discuss personal and professional growth and development. I'm hopeful that by sharing my story, others will feel empowered to contribute honestly as well.

But most important, I do my best to be honest about the challenges I've overcome to show Clayton that doing your best doesn't always mean finding success—and that he shouldn't give up just because he hits a roadblock. I know that Clayton isn't reading my LinkedIn posts, at least not yet. But by being honest with others, and with him, I'm hopeful that he will continue growing into a persistent, resilient, and empathetic young man, perhaps more prepared than I was to confront the challenges that are bound to come his way.

So much of my life is focused on the future. Samantha and I imagine what the future holds for Clayton and SaMya. We have hopes for ourselves, and though we take life day by day, it's exciting to be able to dream about the future.

But the truth is, I'm stuck in between two worlds right now.

Several years ago, when I made contact with my brothers and met my uncles, I believed that a new chapter in my life was set to begin. For so much of my childhood and adolescence, a sense of absence weighed heavily on my heart. My father's absence, of course, but also an emptiness I felt in not having a relationship with my paternal siblings and cousins because of the shame my father felt about me.

Once I made contact with my father and his side of the family, I felt like that absence was going to fade away. I could see my future, and it felt full of life. New memories awaited me, and the family I had yearned for seemed possible.

But none of that happened.

In retrospect, it's not hard for me to see why. The door had been closed for so long, and there was so much shared history among my father's family, a history that hadn't included me. It was too difficult at that stage in our lives for us to forge the kinds of deep connections that keep many families close. My siblings had their own realities. In that reality, their father was around. He went on vacations with them; he showed up to family gatherings. In many ways, he was a family man. So how were they to square that with my reality?

My very existence serves as an indictment of my father's betrayal to their mother, a reminder of his infidelity, and a mockery of the vows he made. Merging those two realities seems not to have been in the cards for me. After that initial meeting, there was little momentum on the part of my siblings and cousins to keep things going. We fell out of touch and I haven't talked to any of them since we first met in Georgia back in 2010. While they occasionally cross my mind, I don't see myself making an effort to reach out again.

Still, old habits die hard.

Shortly after Clayton was born, my mind returned to my father. At the time, I was studying theology at Boston University, discerning ordination in the AME Church. A mentor at one of the churches where I was completing a practicum knew how focused my work was on fatherhood, and he came to the conclusion that the anger and resentment I felt toward my father was stifling me.

"You need to fly to Georgia and tell your father you forgive him," he told me. "Forgive him and release this grip he has on you."

I was willing to try almost anything to free myself from the hurt I still felt, and my theological training supported the notion that forgiveness is essential in any relationship. Plus, I thought about how my father had prevented me from meeting his father, my grandfather, before his death. I didn't want that for Clayton.

I called my father and asked him if he would like to meet his grandson.

"Meet me at the gas station where I used to meet your mom," he told me.

When I told Samantha about our plans, about the baggage-filled location my father chose as the place to meet his grandson, she was appalled. Even then, I understood why she felt this way. But when I told her that this meeting was something I had to do, she supported me.

I put aside my own anger, both lingering from my childhood and renewed by selecting the gas station as a meeting point, and drove with Samantha and Clayton to see my father.

The meeting proved not to be particularly emotional or moving. My father held Clayton for a few minutes. That was that. When it was clear that our roadside meeting was coming to an end, I said something that felt appropriate for the moment—even if it didn't feel sincere.

"Dad, I forgive you," I said.

"For what?" he shot back.

I didn't want to start a fight, pick at old scars, so I refrained from taking the bait.

"Dad, everything's good," I said. "I want you to be a part of Clayton's life."

We said goodbye, with no plans in place to meet again, but I also left the door to a relationship ajar, even if only a crack. On the way to our next destination, my cellphone rang. It was my father. Perhaps he wanted to reciprocate the offer.

"I don't know who you think you were talking to back there," he said, indignation coloring his words. "I'm not one of those busted-ass men you work with on the streets. I bought you school clothes when you were a kid."

A pause.

"I'm your father!"

During my entire life, I never heard my father exhibit an inkling of self-awareness or engage in any meaningful moments of self-reflection. But that moment on the phone was revelatory. He showed that he believed he had done nothing wrong. He pointed to his purchase of shirts and pants, many years earlier, as proof that he was a good dad. And he believed that he was a father to me. At that point, I realized that my father was battling his own demons—and accepted that they had little to do with me. That chapter of my life had ended.

We haven't spoken since.

Mom's world today is smaller than it used to be. She reads her Bible, gets to church every Sunday, and sings in the choir when she's feeling up to it. She brags about me to friends at every opportunity and occasionally spends time with her sister, Diane. But she still clings to a version of reality that baffles me. She waits by the phone, and she and my father still spend hours talking.

I've come to accept that my mother's friendship with my father might not make sense to anyone but the two of them, but it does seem to be based in love. My mother occasionally asks me if I've spoken to my father. When she does, Samantha and I shoot each other a quick glance.

"No, Mom," I say, gently.

Samantha and I recently moved from Boston to the Atlanta area, in part so we can expand Fathers' UpLift down here and in part to be closer to family to give our children a relationship with their grandmother before it's too late. I'm no longer angry when Mom chooses my father's phone calls over spending time with me. I have to chalk it up to grace, because otherwise, it's inexplicable. My mother still believes she has done nothing wrong, even if things didn't work out the way she had hoped. She thinks the same about my father. The world they've created for themselves is strange to me, but they remain present for each other, even if they both failed in their own ways to be present to their son.

As I was writing this, one night in my study I flipped through the pages of my well-worn Bible, its spine creased from years of use. I landed on a familiar Gospel passage: "Judge not, that you be not judged" (Matthew 7:1). The words echoed in my mind. My mother had committed a series of transgressions that, to many, feel unforgivable. But not for me.

I thought about forgiveness, who decides who is worthy of it, and instead of recalling the various shortcomings of my mother, I thought of my own. How badly I handled my emotions during Samantha's pregnancy with Clayton. The fights I picked, how I put our marriage at risk.

Accountability is a double-edged sword. It's easy to become ensnared in the belief that to point fingers is a show of strength, when, in truth, it's really a display of insecurity. I have seen this in my mother, a flawed yet loving woman who has shaped me into the man I am today. Sure, there were imperfections, and I am still working my way through the fallouts associated with her decisions, but there was also love. Somehow, these two realities, the grace and the anguish, coexist peacefully in how I interpret my story, and these experiences shape how I help other men heal.

I love and deeply respect my mother, but I'm at a place in my life where I am ready to accept things the way they are rather than engage in a futile attempt to change things that I have no power to control. I cannot buy back those years when I yearned for my father to be with my mom and me, and I don't want to continue making the same mistakes today. I've never told my mother directly that I forgive her, how her actions made me feel. And I'm not sure I ever will, because I've come to understand how much I don't understand about her. Her seizures can be brought on by stress, and I don't want to hurt her. We've reached an understanding and that might be enough for us.

Still, the world that could have been grips my imagination. It was my focus, perhaps even my obsession, for many years. But I've also learned that by shifting my focus from what is absent in my life to what is present, I continue to heal, even if that process doesn't look like what I had long imagined for myself. I am married to a funny, beautiful, loving woman, together with whom I am raising two bright, empathetic, and lively children. I'm able to give my children and my wife the kind of life I desperately wanted for myself when I was a child, and that is a gift I never could have imagined giving when I was focused almost exclusively on what I didn't have. Learning to embrace abundance is a lesson that took many years, but one that I hold tightly to today.

This is perhaps not the perfect ending to this chapter of my life, but it's the right one. It's the ending that created this version of myself, and the one that has prompted me to see more clearly the many men in my life who were fathers to me all along. By focusing more on my angels, and less on my deficits, I see much more clearly how blessed I am.

For all that, I'm grateful.

> **Lesson:** The response creates the pathway. Be mindful of how you react to the student's setbacks. Your response can either propel them forward or cause damage. Your actions set the tone.

EPILOGUE

My admiration for President Barack Obama goes all the way back to college, when I volunteered to staff his campaign during a visit to Cookman. I never made it into the venue that day, but I still felt like I had witnessed history. In retrospect, my admiration for the future president had so overwhelmed my psyche that my decision to wear three-piece suits in the stifling Florida humidity was probably an attempt to mirror his suave style.

Which is all to say, President Obama has been an outsize figure in my life since I devoured *Dreams from My Father* and read how he not only coped with not having his father present in his life, but went on to thrive as a successful political leader, loving husband, and involved father. When he ran for president, I saw in his example a source of motivation for myself.

Fast forward to 2018, when the Obama Foundation was launching an inaugural fellowship program, designed to empower young social changemakers to take their ideas and run with them. At this point, Fathers' UpLift was thriving, and while Samantha and I were still hustling every day to make sure our work continued, we were fortunate to have just enough space to envision the future. We wanted Fathers' Up-Lift to grow and expand, but we knew we'd have to grow our networks for this to happen.

When I approached Samantha with the idea of applying to be an Obama Fellow, she was encouraging if a bit skeptical. We were both busy professionals, raising a child together, and she saw how much work went into a fellowship application process, often without much in return. I had been fortunate to gain some valuable skills in previous fellowships, but the challenge of me spending more time away from home was something we both had to take seriously. But as she always does, Samantha told me to follow my heart and if I felt called to apply, I should.

So I did—along with 20,000 other people from more than 190 countries. I made it through several rounds in the application process, and I tried to psych myself up for the in-person interview. When the day arrived, I rehearsed my talking points, took a deep breath, and did my best to explain my vision for Fathers' UpLift. Satisfied with the conversation, I left and waited for the next steps. When an invitation didn't materialize, I was devastated.

But Samantha and I had so much work to do at Fathers' UpLift, not to mention raising Clayton, that I didn't dwell on my failed application for too long. But the following year, three people each said the same thing to me.

"You should apply again."

I believe God speaks in threes, so I took that as a sign. And why not? The story of my life up to that point had been a series of fumbles, followed by short completions, and eventually, touchdowns. Few people get everything they want the first time they try for it, but too many people give up after an initial obstacle. I wasn't going to let a wounded ego get in the way of possibly tapping into a robust network to help me gain the skills I needed to grow Fathers' UpLift. The work was too important and there were men counting on me. I went ahead and applied again.

Three things stand out from that second time I interviewed.

First, I was a year older and was able to draw on all the work we had accomplished during that year. I turned those experiences into anecdotes that got to the heart of what Samantha and I were doing at Fathers' UpLift, particularly how helping disadvantaged men to be good fathers was a bigger goal than any one person or organization. Second, I experienced a healthy and consoling sense of detachment from the process. The first year, I had built up the possibility of a fellowship so much, I thought my future and the future of Fathers' UpLift depended on it. But when I reapplied, I realized that while the fellowship would be an incredible opportunity, I also remembered that our work would continue either way. We had done amazing work in the year following my rejection, and if I didn't make the cut again this time, we'd get back to our mission. Finally, I reframed how I explained our vision, emphasizing the need for community in order to achieve this work. I think that spoke to the fellowship directors, who responded positively to my pitch. I accepted the invitation to become an Obama Fellow.

Over the course of the next couple of years, I tapped into a network of inspiring, accomplished community activists intent on making the world a more just, fair, and equitable place. I'll never forget that first meeting with former First Lady Michelle Obama. I remember Mrs. Obama congratulating us for being selected as fellows, and even encouraging us to take a moment to let it all soak in. But, she also reminded us that we were where we were because we had stood on the shoulders of others. We should remember that, and bring others into these spaces when given the opportunity.

Executive coaching, which included teaching skills in leadership and fundraising, led to friendships that withstood the challenges of the pandemic and continue to pay dividends today. I also benefited from the power of President Obama's megaphone, which he generously shared with the Obama Fellows. On Father's Day in 2019, Mr. Obama used his Twitter account to highlight Fathers' UpLift.

"Happy Father's Day to Charles, one of our @Obama Foundation Fellows, and all the dads at Fathers' UpLift," the former president tweeted. "Today, we're celebrating fathers like these who provide a powerful example—not only for their kids, but for the rest of us, too."

The post, which has been liked by more than 65,000 people, featured a two-minute video of me talking about Fathers' Up-Lift, explaining our mission, and featuring some of the men we work with. In the days that followed, Samantha and I were flooded with calls and emails, from people seeking help for their families and organizations wanting to learn more about our work. We scrambled to reply to as many requests as possible, recognizing the unique opportunity we had just been given by the former president.

During my fellowship, I also met great dads, men whose life experiences ran a wide range but who were nonetheless present in the lives of their children. That these highly successful and driven men made their children a priority reminded me of the importance of the work we do at Fathers' UpLift.

I remember one visit to Washington, D.C., as part of the fellowship. When I found myself in the gift shop of the Smithsonian National Air and Space Museum, it hit me just how much I missed Clayton. I was there with another fellow, also a young dad, and instead of discussing our work, sort of the default at these kinds of gatherings, we talked about our kids. That's where we both wanted to be, home with our children. I left the gift shop with an armload of toys for Clayton, including a replica of Air Force One that he still has today.

A couple of years later, I was in New York to take part in the Obama Foundation's Democracy Forum, during which President Obama delivered remarks. I hadn't yet been able to meet my role model face-to-face, because of the pandemic, so I was eager to be there in person. During the summit, I paused to reflect on where I was. I had grown up the son of a single mother, the grandson of a woman who cleaned houses for the wealthy. I had struggled with the circumstances of my life, at one point even wondering if I had the will to go on. But here I was, in the same room as a former president of the United States. If there was ever a moment in my professional life that gave me pause, this was it.

Part of the fellowship experience included an exercise where we wrote down our goals for our two years at the Foundation. Without question, my first goal was as specific as it was aspirational: to be featured in a TED Talk, which I saw as an opportunity to bring the message of Fathers' UpLift to as wide an audience as possible.

I love public speaking, and any time I have a mic in front of me, I'm eager to talk about the successes at Fathers' UpLift, to highlight the life-changing work my team, Samantha, and I engage in every day. TED had hosted a regional event in Boston a number of years earlier, and I applied, but I wasn't chosen.

But I continued to nurture that goal and thought, *Why not see what this new network can do?*

As I wrapped up my time as a fellow, I learned that the woman who had interviewed me, both the first time and the second, was connected to TED. She generously offered to introduce me to folks there, and I was given a chance to apply to give a talk.

"Charles, what do you want to talk about?" I remember being asked during the interview.

"I want to talk about fatherhood," I said.

They were intrigued and asked me to share more of my story.

Over the next several months, I worked with TED to sharpen my story and distill it down to the most pertinent points. Samantha and Clayton grew tired of hearing me rehearse, but they remained supportive and upbeat about it all. Producers contacted the people I would mention in my talk to get their permission to include them in my story. Because my work is so intimately tied to my personal life, this meant members of my family would have to sign off on being included.

When the day of the talk arrived, I flew to Palm Springs, California, and found myself in a green room backstage. I practiced my story in my head, recalling the points I wanted to highlight, and spent extra time practicing the moments that are still difficult for me to get through. I had a compassionate and talented storytelling coach, but I was still nervous as hell. At TED, everything has to be committed to memory, and even though I knew my story better than anyone else, telling it to a large crowd of strangers, in front of a camera, would be an ordeal. A dreaded bout of impostor syndrome showed up at the worst possible moment, causing me to trip, quite literally, as I walked up the stairs and onto the stage.

Dressed in a navy suit and white button-down shirt, standing in front of a glittery red set with the TED logo behind me, I took a deep breath and started my talk.

"Did you know that an estimated ten million children in the United States see their fathers less than once a month?" I began. "Poverty rates double, emotional and behavioral health issues increase, high school dropout rates increase, as do crime and prison rates."

In some ways, these parts of the talk were easy—facts and figures I had committed to memory, which I had highlighted many times over the course of my career.

But as I stood on that stage, gazing out into the audience and talking about my own life, how my mother had raised me on her own, how each day before school, she would look me in the eyes and say to me, "You are tall, dark, and handsome," my emotions got the better of me. My eyes welled up, my voice broke, and the audience cheered me on to show me the kind of love and support that are critical in situations like these. I regained my poise and continued on with my talk.

I told the story about how Samantha and I created Fathers' UpLift, highlighted some of our successes, and then, inspired by one of my childhood heroes, Mr. Rogers, I urged the audience to consider the angels in their own lives.

"Take a moment with me. Fifteen seconds. And I'll keep the time," I said. "Think about the people who loved you when you lost your way. Who hugged you when you needed it. Who assumed best intentions. Who validated you. And embraced you even when you felt undeserving. Whoever came to mind, try, just try and be that to someone else."

Once the video of the talk appeared online, it was clear that the story had struck a chord. Nearly two million people viewed it, and the story of Fathers' UpLift continues to inspire and challenge. Samantha and I have long planned to grow our organization, and we recently took the next step, moving to the Atlanta area to establish another center. I continue to run the location in Boston, which means more time away from Samantha, Clayton, and SaMya, but it's a sacrifice our family is willing to make. Too many lives are at stake for us to rest comfortably.

For me, I still make it a point to regularly spend fifteen seconds or so thinking of the people who loved me when I needed it most. My mom, who did her best for me despite overwhelming odds stacked against her. Of Samantha, who has been a loving and supportive partner, encouraging me when I'm down and daring me to dream bigger about my own life. Uncle Larry, who didn't waver when my mom leaned on him for help when I felt like my future was at stake. My cousin Ant, who taught me what it means to be a man. Of the many men who acted as father figures in my life.

Then there are the dads whom I've met through Fathers' UpLift. There's Sean, whose face I can still see clearly, tense with worry, as he dialed the digits on my office phone, taking the first step to reconnect with his son. George, whose struggles with self-esteem and his physical health made him think he'd never be a good dad to his daughter, whom he never stopped loving. And Zephaniah, who couldn't forgive the world for taking his beautiful daughter and then himself for how he failed his family in the wake of the tragedy, but who learned to heal and reunited with his wife and surviving children. Each of these dads, and many more, have reminded me of the importance of forgiveness, patience, and endurance. We're all on a unique journey, but by sharing our struggles and accomplishments, we can help make it that much easier.

———

A few months ago, Samantha, Clayton, SaMya, and I were at a McDonald's near Atlanta. Clayton is obsessed with McDonald's fries, and sometimes it feels like they're the only thing he'll eat without a battle. So we occasionally give in and let him enjoy their salty goodness.

With a bag of fries in hand, I began to drive away when Clayton started crying. I looked around and didn't see any reason for him to be upset, so I asked what was wrong.

"That man, he's homeless, and we gotta help him," Clayton said through tears. "Can you give him some money?"

I was startled by Clayton's reaction to seeing the man. We had spent enough time in cities that seeing people in distress wasn't, sadly, a novel experience for Clayton. But clearly something moved him in this instance.

"I don't have any money," I told him. "But how about we go to an ATM and I'll get some cash."

I drove down the street, withdrew some money, and handed Clayton a few dollars. We drove back to the young man. Clayton rolled down his window and handed over the money. He instantly felt better.

Before Clayton was born, I was terrified about becoming a father. I couldn't move on from the fact that my own dad had not been present in my life, and I was attached to the deficits his absence had caused. Even though I knew better, I felt that because of my dad's absence, I was consigned by fate to being a bad father. I just knew that I would pass on the worst of myself to my son, condemning him to a similar fate. I couldn't see how I would break the cycle.

Over the years, as I've come to accept that my past does not dictate my future, I've dropped that mentality. With each milestone in Clayton's and SaMya's lives, I offer a prayer of gratitude that I am able to be here for these moments, to help them explore the world and to create a reality for them that is based in love.

That day at McDonald's was one of those moments. I saw in my son a strong and compassionate heart, his desire to want to make a difference in the life of a stranger. My son is growing into a kind, compassionate young man. I know that like everyone else, he will face struggles and challenges, and no matter how hard Samantha and I try to protect him, he will occasionally get hurt. But I also know that my son will feel supported and loved by his father, and that for as long as I am here, he can always count on me to be present.

ACKNOWLEDGMENTS

I thank my team for holding me during this process. Your care, guidance, and coaching have meant the world to me. I appreciate you taking a chance on me, Samantha Fils-Daniels, Paula Stone Williams, Michael O'Loughlin, and Roger Freet.

I would like to also express my deepest gratitude to the Fils, Marshall, and Thomas families for your unyielding support and love. You have been my steadfast rock through challenges and triumphs alike, and I truly appreciate everything you've done for me.

NOTES

1. Charles C. Daniels, "Evidence Informed Fatherhood Program: An Evaluation," *Journal of Social Work* 23, no. 2 (2023): 221–42. See also Susan Yoon et al., "Father Involvement and Behavior Problems Among Preadolescents at Risk of Maltreatment," *Journal of Child and Family Studies* 27 (2018): 494–504.
2. Keon L. Gilbert et al., "Visible and Invisible Trends in Black Men's Health: Pitfalls and Promises for Addressing Racial, Ethnic, and Gender Inequities in Health," *Annual Review of Public Health* 37 (2016): 295–311.
3. *Ring the Alarm: The Crisis of Black Youth Suicide in America* (Congressional Black Caucus Emergency Taskforce on Black Youth Suicide and Mental Health, 2019), https://watsoncoleman.house .gov/suicidetaskforce.
4. *A Shared Sentence: The Devastating Toll of Parental Incarceration on Kids, Families and Communities,* (Annie E. Casey Foundation, Kids Count, 2016), https://assets.aecf.org/m/resourcedoc/aecf -asharedsentence-2016.pdf.
5. John Gramlich, "Black Imprisonment Rate in the U.S. Has Fallen by a Third Since 2006," Pew Research Center, May 6, 2020, https://www.pewresearch.org/short-reads/2020/05/06/share-of -black-white-hispanic-americans-in-prison-2018-vs-2006.

6. Jessica Tollestrup, *Fatherhood Initiatives: Connecting Fathers to Their Children* (Congressional Research Service, 2018), https://crsreports.congress.gov/product/details?prodcode=RL31025.

7. American Psychiatric Association, *Diagnostic and Statistical Manual of Mental Disorders*, 5th ed. (Arlington, Va.: APA, 2013).

8. Anthony S. Zannas et al., "Epigenetics of Posttraumatic Stress Disorder: Current Evidence, Challenges, and Future Directions," *Biological Psychiatry* 78, no. 5 (2015): 327–35.

9. Charles Daniels Jr. and Samantha Fils Daniels, interview by Tavis Smiley, *Tavis Smiley*, KBLA 1580, October 19, 2022.

10. Daniel Patrick Moynihan, *The Negro Family: The Case for National Action* (U.S. Department of Labor, Office of Policy Planning and Review, 1965), https://www.dol.gov/general/aboutdol/history/webid-moynihan.

11. Ibid.

12. Joy DeGruy-Leary, *Post Traumatic Slave Syndrome: America's Legacy of Enduring Injury and Healing* revised ed. (Joy DeGruy Publications, 2017).

13. Ibid.

14. Jahdziah St. Julien, *A Portrait of Caring Black Men* (New America, 2021), https://www.newamerica.org/better-life-lab/reports/portrait-caring-black-men.

15. Ibid.

16. Juliana Menasce Horowitz et al., "Race in America 2019," Pew Research Center, April 9, 2019, https://www.pewresearch.org/social-trends/2019/04/09/race-in-america-2019.

17. Terris Todd, "What Absent Fathers Need to Do Right Now for Their Children," Fox News, October 3, 2021, https://www.foxnews.com/opinion/absent-fathers-children-terris-todd.

18. Bruce D. Perry, "Examining Child Maltreatment Through a Neurodevelopmental Lens: Clinical Applications of the Neurosequential Model of Therapeutics," *Journal of Loss and Trauma* 14, no. 4 (2009): 240–55.

19. Vincent J. Felitti et al., "Relationship of Childhood Abuse and Household Dysfunction to Many of the Leading Causes of Death in Adults," *American Journal of Preventive Medicine* 14, no. 4 (1998): 245–58.

20. Daniel P. Chapman et al., "Adverse Childhood Experiences and the Risk of Depressive Disorders in Adulthood," *Journal of Affective Disorders* 82, no. 2 (2004): 217–25.

21. Daniel J. Pilowsky et al., "Adverse Childhood Events and Lifetime Alcohol Dependence," *American Journal of Public Health* 99, no. 2 (2009): 258–63.

22. Selma Fraiberg et al., "Ghosts in the Nursery. A Psychoanalytic Approach to the Problems of Impaired Infant-Mother Relationships," *Journal of the American Academy of Child Psychiatry* 14, no. 3 (1975): 387–421.

23. Katie N. Russell et al., "Exploring Low-Income, Black Fathers' Strengths and Barriers to Positive Change Using Qualitative Methods," *Family Relations* 73, no. 3 (2024): 1799–1822.

24. Abigail Henson, "'The Biggest Thing You Can Rob Is Somebody's Time': Exploring How the Carceral State Bankrupts Fathers Through Temporal Debt," *Punishment & Society* 26, no. 1 (2024): 53–71.

25. D. L. Hoyert, *Maternal Mortality Rates in the United States, 2023* (Centers for Disease Control and Prevention, National Center for Health Statistics, 2023), https://www.cdc.gov/nchs/data/hestat/maternal-mortality/2023/Estat-maternal-mortality.pdf.

26. Wendy Sawyer and Peter Wagner, *Mass Incarceration: The Whole Pie 2024* (Prison Policy Initiative, 2024), https://www.prisonpolicy.org/reports/pie2024.html.

27. Julie Wertheimer, "Racial Disparities Persist in Many U.S. Jails," *Pew*, May 16, 2023, https://www.pewtrusts.org/en/research-and-analysis/issue-briefs/2023/05/racial-disparities-persist-in-many-us-jails.

28. Mariel Alper et al., *2018 Update on Prisoner Recidivism: A 9-Year*

Follow-up Period (2005–2014) (U.S. Department of Justice, Bureau of Justice Statistics, 2018), https://bjs.ojp.gov/content/pub/pdf/18upr9yfupo514.pdf.

29. Annalies Goger et al., "Prisoner Reentry," in *A Better Path Forward for Criminal Justice* (Brookings Institution, 2021), https://www.brookings.edu/articles/a-better-path-forward-for-criminal-justice-prisoner-reentry.

30. Nestor Ramos and Evan Allen, "Life and Loss on Methadone Mile," *Boston Globe*, July 2016, https://apps.bostonglobe.com/graphics/2016/07/methadone-mile.

31. Data Tool: "Demographics of the U.S. Psychology Workforce," American Psychological Association, 2022. https://www.apa.org/workforce/data-tools/demographics.

CHARLES C. DANIELS JR., PHD, is a dynamic leader and co-founder of Fathers' UpLift, a nonprofit organization dedicated to supporting fathers and strengthening families. His own experience of growing up without a father shaped his life's mission. Raised by his loving mother, Dr. Daniels went on a journey of self-discovery that revealed a powerful truth: He was not to blame for his father's choices. This understanding ignited his commitment to help others navigate similar struggles.

An accomplished therapist, Dr. Daniels holds a bachelor's degree from Bethune-Cookman University and a master's degree in divinity from the Boston University School of Theology. He also earned a master's in social work and a PhD from Simmons University's School of Social Work. His insights and advocacy have reached millions through appearances on platforms such as CNN, ABC, and *Good Morning America*. In recognition of his innovative approach to addressing critical societal issues, he was honored as one of twenty Obama Foundation Fellows worldwide in 2019, distinguishing himself as a civic innovator dedicated to transformational change.

Alongside his wife, Samantha Fils-Daniels, with whom he co-founded Fathers' UpLift, Dr. Daniels is a devoted father to two children, Clayton and SaMya. Together, they embody the essence of family and hope, working tirelessly to uplift fathers and empower future generations.

ABOUT THE TYPE

This book was set in Dante, a typeface designed by Giovanni Mardersteig (1892–1977). Conceived as a private type for the Officina Bodoni in Verona, Italy, Dante was originally cut only for hand composition by Charles Malin, the famous Parisian punch cutter, between 1946 and 1952. Its first use was in an edition of Boccaccio's *Trattatello in laude di Dante* that appeared in 1954. The Monotype Corporation's version of Dante followed in 1957. Though modeled on the Aldine type used for Pietro Cardinal Bembo's treatise *De Aetna* in 1495, Dante is a thoroughly modern interpretation of that venerable face.